Wendy ⇗
I hope y
I wish you —
Peace, Love & Happiness ☺.
Blair & (Shepkie)

soulitude

SOULITUDE

Copyright © 2018 by R. B. Brown

Tellwell Talent
www.tellwell.ca

ISBN
978-0-2288-0248-8 (Hardcover)
978-0-2288-0246-4 (Paperback)
978-0-2288-0247-1 (eBook)

Introduction

My wife of sixty years passed in April of 2017. I don't have to describe the unbearable grief associated with such a traumatic happening since everyone has had some similar experience. We had talked many times about death and dying and what really happens to us when that day arrives. Shyrlie and I believed in an afterlife and had numerous readings from mediums over the years. We had even made a pact to leave together when the time came, no long-term care facilities, hospitals, or doctors for us. When that time did come for Shyrlie, circumstances denied the fulfilment of our pact. I have to stay here and Shyrlie tells me I'll be here for some time.

Shyrlie was ill for several years with creeping dementia, as I called it. I took care of her at our home with help from our daughter, Lori. Our eldest daughter, Vicki, lives in Ontario and was taking treatment herself. James, our son, was dealing with the situation in his own way. Caring for Shyrlie at home wasn't the easiest undertaking, but I knew she was happier in familiar surroundings. Finally, at noon on April 18th, Shyrlie left, and it doesn't matter what you believe in: it hurts when you lose a partner of sixty years. As I fought my grief I thought of the afterlife, and then I attempted something I shouldn't have - I contacted a medium whom I know quite well and requested a reading. Although I was desperate to talk to Shyrlie, I think my true reason for contacting the medium was to find out if there really is an afterlife and was Shyrlie there. It didn't matter that I truly believed in the afterlife; I had to know if my wife was there and if she was okay. Rita gave me a reading over my old land-line phone on April 26th, just eight days after Shyrl passed. My parents came through, as did an uncle I had never met, and even my grandfather – they all showed up to support me! Having them come through specifically for support was pretty strong verification, but I still wanted to know if Shyrlie was there. Perhaps Shyrlie wasn't able to communicate with me this early after her passing. I didn't know how this was supposed to work from that end.

I asked Rita about Shyrlie and she said that my wife was there, watching how the process of contacting was done! Rita told me that it was quite unusual for someone to communicate that soon. Shyrlie and I had a great talk, and our communication finally put my soul at ease. It was comforting to know I hadn't lost Shyrlie. Rita indicated that Shyrl smiled a lot and her eyes and face were radiant. Shyrl said she didn't want to become a cabbage here on earth. You could say that these were generic responses and could be applied to anyone, and you would be correct. However, I will now cite a couple of comments Rita attributes to Shyrlie and you decide. Keep in mind that these readings took place over a landline phone.

[1] - The day before I had this first reading, our daughter Lori and I were discussing some type of memorial for Shyrlie. A walking trail had been made along the old railway line that ran beside the water of the bay and Shyrl had loved taking strolls beside the water. Lori and I had talked about placing a bench somewhere along the walk where people could sit and enjoy the quietness. At the end of the reading the next day, Shyrl said that if we were considering a memorial she liked the idea of the bench with her name on it. She though it would be both useful and enjoyable!

[2] - During a reading on September 27th, 2017, I asked how Shyrl liked the bench (the bench which Rita had never seen). Rita told us

Shyrlie was embarrassed but loves it, *especially the pictures of her. She says they make her look young.* [We had two pictures of her when she would have been in her forties, I suppose, placed on the large stone at one end of the rose granite bench.]

[3] - I happened to be shopping in Yarmouth a few days before a scheduled reading with Rita. At that time, I was wearing my hair quite long and it was getting in my eyes. For some reason I decided that day I would get it cut. I fortunately found a lady that would do it that morning and she cut and styled it for me. In the middle of the reading three days after my trip to Yarmouth, Shyrlie said, *'I like your haircut!'* Rita had told me that all afflictions suffered here are gone when you enter the afterlife and obviously Shyrl's dementia was no more.

Unless Rita is able to do remote viewing, which she can't, what I have told you has to be the unquestioning truth that I am receiving information from my wife's *soul.* Her validation couldn't be more definitive. There were many more such instances over the past year. She hasn't yet made a comment on the book so I don't know if it is good or bad. She *has* told me, through Rita, that she is proud of me.

In late summer of last year, I was drinking coffee and contemplating the afterlife when it came to me: Hey! If we don't die ... how can there be murder? I kept the question alive for several months, rolling it around in my mind and arguing with myself as to whether my idea was cockeyed or made sense, and would it make a good story While having another reading with Rita, Shyrlie told me to write the book! Who am I to argue?

I believe we all have a soul and that it defines who we are, and that we are here to do positive things for our little corner of the world. I believe in the afterlife and that belief has kept me calm in *most* situations.

I will tell you that Lucas' pain was my pain. It was real and continued for a long time, and I believed in the soul, and that we don't die, and the afterlife. It still took a while for me to get over most of the selfishness of grief. It's never completely gone.

My purpose in writing this book is to help persuade the reader to keep an open mind, investigate all things paranormal and, most importantly. dispel the fear of death and dying. Don't believe me; search for the truth yourself. I did and will be forever blessed for doing so. I wish you peace, love, and happiness.

R. B. Brown
Barrington Passage
Nova Scotia

Forward

Ironically, the age of the internet has offered us access to a wealth and also a dearth of information. As a result we are becoming more astute at undertaking our own research as we are often presented with 'evidence' supporting opposing views.

I hope this book will stir an interest in your own research and ignite your natural instincts to 'feel' what is right for you.

Everyone reading this book, *I feel*, will have, at one time, met a person and felt immediately comfortable or uncomfortable. Our very language itself includes phrases like 'I got a good vibe,' or 'I have a bad vibe.' 'I have a funny feeling,' or 'it didn't feel right.' How many houses were bought because it 'felt like *the one* ' or plans changed because of a 'bad vibe' or a ' funny feeling?'

We are all energetic beings naturally connected to the energy of people, places, things, animals, indeed all life forces. How many will have spoken to someone on the phone who is saying they are fine, but you '*know*' by the tone of their voice that something isn't right? Many will know when others are not being truthful. These instincts are natural and when we connect with them our lives become more harmonious. In the age of technology many have just forgotten how to trust this connection.

In all nations since time began, the continuation of life after leaving this plane, is documented; drawn on cave walls and parchments and told of in stories. Whilst there are a myriad of 'what happens next' descriptions, it is evident that regardless of where in the world, from the most remote tribe to the largest city, the message is the same - when we 'die' it is not the end. In a time when the internet did not exist or missionaries and holy seers had not traversed this plane, all cultures had the same belief. That in its self should spark an interest in us all, to ask ' why is that so'?

The other commonality across all cultures and throughout time is the mention of mystics, psychics, seers, healers, etc, a universally held belief, that is again, in its self, interesting. The very group of scientists who set out to 'disprove' the possibility of this, are now some of the greatest proponents as they seek to explain in complex scientific terms, the same thing the ancients have always said; *we are energetic beings and all connected*' ; a bit like the internet, its all there, connected, like 'one' ; we just need a good search engine, good 'fire-walls' and a good 'spam' filter. Science has known for eons that energy can not be destroyed it can only be transmuted [changed]. We are energy, ergo we will always exist, it can be no other way. It is for you to decide what that looks like for you.

Since a very young age I was aware of energy, and spirit. I did not think it was unusual to see ' people' walk down the hall that were semi transparent or to hear muted conversations; to know what people were feeling or to ' know' what a family member who had passed wanted to say. All babies and children are very connected to that energy. Watch them as they follow something invisible across the room or look up from a crib when they can't see you and they giggle or chatter. They are seeing people, who to them look as real and physical as you or me.

It was only attending school age nine or ten and having a discussion about why someone was doing something I had seen that it was clear that not everyone had the same experiences, as me. I became far quieter about those matters, as school was tough enough.

I remember looking at ants and wondering how many beings were looking at me and wondering how many 'me's' existed, thinking perhaps that for every decision I made there was a 'me' who chose the other path, and wondered if I could ever, see that [something that an arm of science is exploring now]. My family just looked perplexed and whilst not encouraging me, did not discourage these thoughts and expressions.

At age twelve I bought a book on Astral travel. At the time there was not the wealth of books on spirit and connection that there is now, and my interest and connections continued to blossom. By nineteen I was sharing insights from spirit with others and by early twenties I had been guided to a group of mediums and healers who helped me expand my consciousness and connect with love and develop my abilities. To all those people I am eternally grateful.

The purpose of my connection is to bring peace and comfort to those in need. With humor I tell my clients I can not predict the lotto numbers, otherwise I'd be giving sessions by satellite from the Seychelles! I do not float about the room nor does my face and voice change. It is all done in the light and with love. I don't know or wish to know details of anyone's private life as that's their business. As long as the message makes sense that's all I am interested in. I never ask them anything, not even where they are from or why they are here.

All I require from a client is they speak 'yes, no, makes sense, not sure.' The voice vibration of the person being read helps connect. It is like a phone call, nodding your head wont suffice. Clients can be anywhere in the world and we can be face to face, on a phone or via the net it matters not, as distance means nothing to the spirit. I always ask that the client receives information they need to validate something they could not know, perhaps about a physical attribute of a person passed over, or something that is being planned that has not yet come to pass. This then helps with trusting the communication even more. I often receive calls and messages from excited clients, after the sessions confirming details of the reading which I have usually forgotten, as its not mine to know. I have given messages to judges, doctors, CEOs, religious ministers and people from all walks of life and race. The one common thread is love, and the messages bring comfort and often guidance for that person or family member presently in their life.

Sometimes there have been sessions where for my learning, or because of the intensity, I have remembered. One such session in my early days with clients was with a mother and her youngest son who arrived upset without an appointment on my door step. I knew it was important to see them. As we sat together I saw and felt her other son, a man in his early twenties. All this young man would say is 'tell my mum I have my trainers [*runners*] on, Tell my mum I have my trainers on.' I was questioning him [*with my inner voice*] to tell me his name, how he passed- something to give me some depth of information to help his family. He was insistent about the message, so I passed it on word for word and they both dissolved in tears.

He then told me quickly he'd passed in a car crash. He passed at the scene and needed to be cut out of the vehicle. He had suffered trauma to his face and he showed me his now perfect teeth. He provided a lot of information regarding the accident. I saw him in jeans and a soccer shirt and white trainers which was all confirmed and the songs played at the funeral and what had been done in his memory. When the mother had composed herself a little she explained that he was cremated, and was wearing his jeans and his new soccer top but the crematorium had not allowed the footwear as they said it was not environmentally permitted. She had been devastated thinking she had not 'sent him off properly'. The session then became relaxed and there was lots of smiles and some laughter amidst the tears. She said the comfort it had brought was immeasurable for her and her youngest son. That session taught me just to pass on what I get, without judgment and that the simplest of messages can have the greatest impact.

My descriptions of family members, personalities and physical attributes such as specific scars make peoples jaws drop in astonishment. Names, dates, certain phrases both known and those checked have brought many people back for additional sessions.

A lady recently sat down and immediately her mother came through. The first words from her mother where *I am sorry I left before you got there, but if you had been there I would have found it even harder to go, so please don't feel guilty. Thank you for taking my hand. I love you too and I will see your granddaughter. I have already".* The client had missed her mothers passing by about 10 minutes and had taken her hand, told her mother that she loved her and said 'You wont see my grand child.' At the time of the sitting the sex of the baby was not known by the soon to be grandma, but as the client sat with me that day, her daughter had found out and wanted her parents and people to know – when the client got home she called me about the baby news in tears of joy and relief, that her mum had seen the little girl and all was well.

Spirit bring many signs to us all, we just need to be open – we smell aromas when there is no explanation; hear a voice call our name; find dimes in odd places- all manner of things. People have had TVs turn on. One gentleman who lived alone got up in the early hours as he couldn't sleep after his wife had passed. He walked into the kitchen to make a drink to find the kettle on already! I always ask if they could possibly vacuum my house or clean the windows, but so far no takers from spirit, I know they appreciate the humor though.

Scientists do not know where our sense of humor resides, they do not know where consciousness resides. There are endless accounts of 'miracles' happening such as people being 'dead' for hours and then awakening; of people 'floating above their bodies' describing the scene usually at an accident or operating theater. One gentleman was able to tell the nurse where they had put his false teeth – something he couldn't have known as he was 'dead' when they removed them and then he watched where they took them, before being revived; the nurse retrieved his teeth.

There are many instances that scientists and medical professional witness are unable to explain with all their training.

Remember, we are all connected. For centuries people sat staring into fires, or gazing at stars, communicating with their ancestors, being alive to their instincts, and understanding the 'messages' and 'signs'. In our race to *progress* we are only now realizing we allowed our culture to be pushed aside and left out of our lives. But we are coming full circle. Scientists are echoing ancient teachings, enthused like children discovering something for the first time. Long may it continue and may technology be developed to 'prove' what has always been felt and always been known by those who kept the conscious connection.

In truth we all know everything. We always have, we just need to remember.

I hope this book helps *you* remember, and inspires you to journey where your instincts lead.

Rita Crosbie
Clairvoyant, Clairsentient, Medium, Sound
Healer, Life Coach, Inspirational Speaker

soulitude

R.B. Brown

• • • • •

Every book has a soul; the soul of the person who wrote it
and the soul of those who read it and dream about it.
- Carlos Ruiz Zafon

Lucas McNab stood at the kitchen sink, his hands gripping the counter, shoulders hunched, head bowed as if in submission. He was in memory again, in the misty time of years passed, happy years that had ended too soon. His eyes moved slowly to the side and saw the drain tray with the ever present plate, knife, fork, spoon, and cup. Only one of each, and the constant reminder that he was now alone. His eyes welled up and a solitary tear fell into the now empty dish pan.

He straightened and stepped away from the sink, leaving the dishes to dry themselves as she had always told him to do whenever he had attempted to dry them. He took a glass from the corner cupboard, walked over to the little liquor cabinet he had built for them years ago, reached in, and took a bottle of scotch by the neck. Then he made his way to the sunroom at the back of the house. He opened the glass door, stepped through, and slowly made his way to one of the leather chairs. Setting the bottle and glass on the side table, he slowly turned and looked at the face in the frame hanging on the wall. It was the smiling face of his beloved wife Sarah, his life partner, his true friend. It was his whole life in that frame.

Sarah's death a few weeks past wasn't a sudden loss to Lucas. She had begun to slowly drift away from him a year or two before that. It slowly developed into a situation where he was living with a stranger … or was he the stranger?

The crushing grief never left him. He could never have imagined the pain that engulfed his heart. The nights were the worst. Mornings too were difficult, but the dark was the loneliest. He put off going upstairs to his empty bed for as long as he could. Each night began the same way: scotch to recall memories of their life together and to feel the hurt of missing her. Scotch to bring on the whisky-induced sleep that would blot out the pain.

The sunroom was a refuge. In the ever-present quiet, he could spend precious moments with Sarah, keeping her close to him. Here he relived his sorrow and her pain. He questioned the care he had given her, always asking himself if he had done all he could, and always answering, no. The guilt he felt was crushing, and it kept him in sorrow. Hours would pass while he filled the little room with grief and memories. He recalled how she loved to walk, especially in the fog. They would hold hands or she would take him by the arm ... he missed her so much.

Eventually, missing a few steps and mumbling banalities, he stumbled up the stairs to his bedroom tomb, removed what clothing he could, and crawled under the covers to suffer another troubled sleep until the morning brought another lonely day.

• • • • •

Lucas heard the radio voices begin the day as they always did. The alarm was permanently tuned to the CBC and the familiar voices lulled him to sleep, or they used to, and regularly woke him up every morning. He worked his tongue in and out of his desert-dry mouth as if it had a life of its own. He grimaced as he attempted to swallow. All just part of his morning ritual after drinking the 'water of life'. That epithet was so wrong and he proved it over and over. Eventually awareness kicked in. He stretched and rolled out of bed.

He pulled on what clothes he had managed to get out of the night before, slid into his mules, and made it safely down to the kitchen. He needed coffee immediately. He perked six cups the old-fashioned way and the aroma in the early morning was comforting. Though the quietness of the house never changed, he couldn't get used to it. He roamed through the house, so devoid of life, wishing he would find her sitting in her favourite easy chair, or dusting the shelves. He longed for her bright smiling face to turn to him and say, lovingly, 'Good morning, dear.' Lucas sensed her at times, or he thought he did. But he knew that wasn't possible. He would be sitting in the living room watching TV, and suddenly he would think Sarah was in the kitchen. These episodes seemed real to him. They had been married forty-two years and their love had become deep and strong, the result of working together to overcome all the usual obstacles that create the memories. But this was not his life anymore. Everything had changed. He felt lost. He felt like he was floating, unable to get his feet back on firm ground. The neighbours had come by with food and condolences, but they eventually left him alone. Everyone at the office had been of great help dropping by with short visits and more food which piled up quickly. Lucas understood their awkwardness in this kind of situation. He hadn't returned to work since the funeral. The firm's owners, Matt Clarke and Wiff Brannigan, had told him to take whatever time he needed. It was a good law firm, and he felt guilty being away so long. Even prior to Sarah's passing his presence at the law firm was intermittent at first but eventually it became full time. Wiff and Matt graciously granted him whatever time he needed.

The coffee, like a transfusion, oozed slowly into his consciousness and brought him back to life. The third cup made him sit up and take notice of the day. It was March. He knew that much. What was the date? He turned to see the calendar page, which confirmed that it was March. He assumed it was most likely the middle of March, with not much real interest. What day it happened to be was even farther out of interest. It didn't make that much difference. It was a nice clear day, blue sky, a rarity for Nova Scotia this winter. It had been cold for several days now, down to minus twelve and fifteen degrees Celsius. It was a constant damp cold that seeped into the bones.

Lucas decided he had to get back to work in some capacity. He would drop in at the firm and catch up on events. It would be good to see familiar faces and talk with someone other than himself. He started to feel better as he cleaned himself up and changed his clothes. 'I don't look too bad for a sixty-niner,' he thought, but when he looked in the mirror he saw a face a lot older than sixty-nine, a face that reflected the agony endured over the past months. Would it get better, he wondered, and did he really care?

A shower and shave improved his outlook for the day. He dressed in grey slacks and socks and chose a cream-coloured dress shirt. Lucas selected a tie from the dozens hanging in their closet and made a feeble attempt to knot it, not really wanting to wear it. The previous weeks, when clothes hadn't mattered a helluva lot, had broken the long-standing dress code for lawyers, and he liked it. The suits, which were his uniform over the many years, now felt phoney and uncomfortable. Tossing the tie on the bed, he took a navy blazer from its hanger and unhurriedly made his way down the stairs. He looked around the kitchen and through the archway into the living room. He and Sarah loved the openness of their house. It allowed a closeness that wrapped around the living areas and held them together. They had shared a dislike for doors. Doors shut you out, or in. Entering the attached garage Lucas took his winter jacket off the hook and threw it over his arm.

He scanned the garage, and there it was. Her car: the little yellow Miata she loved. He swallowed hard to stop the tears from rising and stepped into his Equinox. As he opened the garage door, his eyes were on the Miata, and he pictured her behind the wheel waving to him. Like the sea slowly rising on the beach, the sorrow and longing crept over him. Lucas almost looked forward to the feeling.

After a brief wait for a lull in traffic, Lucas eased onto the Bedford Highway. God, how many times had he made this trip? He and Sarah had lived on Gateway Road for forty of their forty-two years together. They had built their house when there were few houses in the area. Over time their surroundings had developed into a nice, quiet street. He and Sarah had worked hard finishing the house themselves as their funds disappeared, but it was fun work. Nothing put them off back then. Like the song said, 'ten-foot-high and bullet proof': that was him and Sarah. They had each other and that was enough. Those years were good years and Lucas smiled at the memories. As they followed the development of their street and the increase in traffic, how many times had they talked about moving away, always concluding that they really liked Gateway and their neighbours too much to leave and start over somewhere else.

He was passing under the MacKay Bridge, or the 'new bridge' as it was known locally. It had been completed in 1970, seven years before he and Sarah had built their home on Gateway. He admired the huge, soaring construction every time he drove past. Nearly seventy thousand cars used the bridge daily! He glanced quickly at the area under the approach to the bridge to check if there were any 'street people' camped out. He didn't see anyone this morning. As he approached George Street, he looked for somewhere to park. He didn't intend to stay long. Just make his presence known to everyone and show he was still able to sit up and take nourishment.

What a break! Lucas noticed a small delivery van leaving the curb and he eased the SUV into the vacated spot. After feeding the meter, he entered the Toronto Dominion Tower's glass doors and took the elevator to the fourteenth-floor law offices of Brannigan and Clarke. Seeing those names on the brass plate beside the suite's doors brought a sense of belonging. He had turned down their partnership offer several years ago. At the time, he and Sarah had decided to make more time for themselves. What a great decision that turned out to be, though they had no idea how little time they had.

Brannigan and Clarke was a well-respected law firm. Wilfred 'Wiff' Brannigan's father had started the law office in the seventies, turning it over to his son in 2002. Wiff was a portly fifty-four-year old. Matt Clarke was kept on board at the stern urging of Wiff's father. Old man Brannigan was aware of his son's shortcomings and had made sure Matt' experience would be ever-present; he had made Matt a full partner in the firm by including it in his will. Matt was sixty-two. Wiff had no problem with the arrangement. The two men got along fairly well, rather like opposite sides of the same coin.

Lucas had joined the firm immediately after graduating from Dalhousie Law. He was a competent lawyer all right. He earned his income, though it was not large. It had made a comfortable living for him and Sarah, although she had worked most of their marriage too. She was a school teacher of primary classes throughout most of her career. Perhaps these hours spent with five-year-olds had influenced her decision not to have children, as she wanted adult companionship.

Lucas quietly opened the heavy oak door to the reception area. Alison Boudreau was intently reading correspondence with her back to the entrance and didn't take notice of him. He unobtrusively approached her reception desk, leaned toward her, and lightly cleared his throat.

"Lucas! What in the world are you doing here so soon?" she exclaimed, quickly rounding her desk to throw her arms around him and give him an honest hug. "Hey, everyone! Look at what blew in!"

Suddenly, people came scurrying from their offices, converging on the reception area. Walking quickly with an outstretched hand was Wiff Brannigan, a big broad smile on his face.

"Lucas! It's good to see ya. How ya doin', old son! We didn't expect ya back so soon. We told ya to take as much time as ya needed, didn't we?"

"I know you did, Wiff. I just came by to check in and maybe have some intelligent conversation." Lucas smiled. "I got tired of arguing with myself and losing."

"If it's intelligent conversation you're looking for, you'll have to go farther afield than Wiff Brannigan." Matthew Clarke made his way through the small crowd of people who were all laughing and making polite comments. "It's good to see you back, Lucas. How are you making out? It's not easy, I know. Do you need anything? Anything at all?"

Matthew played the perfect opposite of Wiff. He was smooth and accomplished, good with clients who required compassion and a soothing attitude. Lucas liked Matthew more than Wiff, but they were both good friends.

"Thanks, Matt, but I'm good. Just needed to get out of the house for a bit. Keeping my office warm, eh? I don't see Ann anywhere. Is she ill?"

Ann Hughes was Lucas' secretary, assistant really, and he thought it strange she wasn't at the firm.

"Is she still here?" he asked Matt as he looked over the faces of the group.

"Yes, she's still here. I think she's running an errand. Should be back before long. We'll keep her busy until you make it back."

Unnoticed, Alison had sneaked into an empty office to use the telephone. She put through a quick call to an answering service and left a short message.

"Okay, people. Back to what you all were doin." Wiff took Lucas by the arm and steered him to his office.

Matt brought up the rear. "Alison, dear one, could you see we get some coffee, please?"

"Right away, Mr. Clarke."

The three men settled into leather arm chairs, Lucas not as comfortably as the other two. He looked around the office with its oak-paneled walls and geometrically-designed carpet, a little worn in places. The familiar aroma of cleaning material mixed with aftershave and 'bullshit'. Lucas chuckled to himself. It *was* familiar and surprisingly comforting.

"Lucas, boy, you have suffered a god-awful loss," said Wiff. "We know it will take time for ya to heal-up some, not that ya ever completely get over somethin' this heavy. Why it's only been, what, four, five weeks?"

"Just over three," Lucas answered, tracing the pattern in the carpet at his feet with his eyes.

"We want ya back here as soon as yer ready, ya know? But we want ya back as the fightin' lawyer ya are. Ready ta square off in the ring agin, so ta speak."

Matt gave a sidelong scowl at Wiff that only Lucas could see.

"I think what Wiff means is that your office will always be here, ready for you again, when you feel up to it. Our caseload is fairly light right now. We've got a couple of new boys getting their feet wet, and Lord knows they need the practice. So don't feel obligated. It takes time. Give it that time. Okay?"

Alison wheeled in a trolley containing a carafe of hot coffee and mugs with the firm's logo on them. She poured a mug for each, turned, and left.

Lucas took a little milk and held the cup in both hands. A feeling came over him that maybe he had come back to the firm too soon. He found Wiff's condescending bait-shed lingo grating, although well-meant. Matthew was, well, Matthew, unflappable in the extreme. Matt was closer to Lucas' age, a fact which influenced how Lucas thought of the two men. The one person he really wanted to see wasn't there. He came to the conclusion that he really didn't want to be here and probably wouldn't for a while yet. The atmosphere became heavy and he felt trapped.

Matt and Wiff were bringing him up to speed on court cases. He heard 'car accident' and 'sue' several times, but he didn't take in the details. He didn't want to hear about the cases. He felt more like an island in this office than he did anywhere else. He decided that, for the present anyway, being an island suited him fine.

● ● ● ● ●

Intimacy is not purely physical. It is the act of connection with someone so deeply, you feel as if you can see into their soul.
- Rechall Varsos

Lucas arrived back at the house at dusk. After leaving the firm he had stopped at McDonald's for a salad and coffee. It was strange, but he had become aware of the smells in the office building. They hadn't been noticeable three weeks ago, but today they had provoked panic in him. McDonald's atmosphere was nicer. He tossed the car keys on the kitchen table. He had always used the rather large table as a repository for everything imaginable. Sarah would get so exasperated with him, but it never did any good. He looked over the field of debris on the table, trying to discern the salvageable from the trash, and he realized now was not the time.

He had poured the scotch over three ice cubes in his glass when he heard a small knocking on the door. Who in hell could that be, he wondered. Setting the glass down amidst the mess on the table, he made his way to the front door. He unlocked and turned the knob, opening the door a crack, enough to peer out at whoever was there. Then he saw her: Ann Hughes. The one person he truly wanted to see. He opened the door wide and stood there, looking into her eyes, those gorgeous blue-green eyes. Ann returned the stare. Her face showed both concern and relief.

"Ann. Come in, come in. I was hoping to see you at the office. They said you were on an errand It's good to see you!" He had had no contact with Ann since the funeral. He hadn't given her much thought until recently. They had worked together on many cases over the years. Ann was fifty-seven but looked ten years younger. She was a looker and he had admired her many times over the years, but not in the usual 'office relationship' that is joked about. There was a genuine deep … respect, for lack of a better word, between the two. Lucas loved his wife too much to have even considered anything more with Ann. They worked well together and he thought it was this respect that had made the relationship so successful.

"Oh, Lucas!" Ann said. "I wanted to see you so much these past weeks. I just didn't know how to approach you. What you must have been going through." She slowly entered the hallway as he eased back to make room.

He held out his arms and Ann did the same. They hugged for a long time, both feeling the comfort of each other's embrace.

"Alison called about you showing up at the firm and looking for me. Instead of rushing back I decided I would rather see you alone. I hope I did the right thing."

"You did," was all Lucas could say. He needed this moment. He needed to feel the warmth and closeness of this woman. Ann could become a safe harbour where he might repair his heart, if it could be repaired. He felt her hair on his face, the exotic aroma of her shampoo. He didn't want to let her go.

"I just poured myself a scotch, Ann. What can I get you? A glass of wine, perhaps? I have a nice Chilean red and some South African white. You name it."

"I think I'd like to try the red, please." Ann took off her coat, tam, and scarf, and she lay them across one of the kitchen chairs. She asked, "How have you been managing, Lucas?"

"Okay, I guess. I have my days. What do they have you doing at the office?" Lucas realized that him being away from the firm might have put Ann in an awkward situation.

"Matt took me under his wing and created work for me. He kept my salary coming in, for which I am grateful. They keep me busy and feeling useful. Actually, I've been assisting some of the new boys. Everyone understands that this is just until you come back."

Lucas found the bottle of red, pulled the cork, and poured a glass. As he passed it to Ann, he held onto the stem for a fraction of a second, and their hands touched.

"Shall we retire to the sunroom, my lady? Our chairs await!" Lucas followed, as Ann made her way down the hall to the pleasant little room. It had windows on three sides, two skylights, deep green carpeting, and an electric fireplace which Lucas turned on as he stepped inside the door. He remembered the three of them sharing many a good laugh in this room.

As they settled into the soft, cool leather chairs, Lucas raised his glass to Ann, waiting for her to raise her glass in answer. As she did, Lucas looked longingly at her slightly drawn countenance. "To good friends, and the future," Lucas said. Ann didn't say anything, but watched him as he took a quick sip of scotch.

They were both silent for a time, with neither one looking at the other. Small talk had no place in the moment. It was almost awkward, and Ann wondered if perhaps it was too soon to make an intrusion into the emptiness she knew he must be experiencing. Maybe Lucas' grief was still too new. She sipped her wine.

"Lucas, I want you to know that I will always be here for you. If you just want to talk, call me. If you don't want to be alone, call me. The three of us go back a long way, and I'm positive Sarah would appreciate and agree with my helping you through your grief."

Slowly raising his head with a quizzical look on his face, he turned to Ann. "What do you mean, Ann, 'Sarah would appreciate and agree'?"

"Oh, Lucas, I'm so sorry I said that." Ann could have kicked herself for referring to his wife in such an off-handed way. "It was just a figure of speech and insensitive of me. Please forgive me, Lucas."

"It's okay, Ann. It just took me by surprise, that's all." He smiled at Ann to show her there were no hard feelings on his part. The very last thing he wanted was to alienate their relationship, the very thing he depended on to keep him anchored in these rough, uncharted seas of loneliness and despair. He raised his glass to her. "Thanks for coming by, Ann. I really appreciate your concern. I've missed you since the funeral." He set down his glass on the little round table between two leather chairs.

Ann looked at the man across from her, her 'boss' for so many years. Images came to her mind of good times shared with him and Sarah. There was never anything between she and Lucas except a deep friendship. It was special, and Sarah recognized it for what it was, she was sure. She so wanted to help him as he suffered through his loss. All she could do for the present was to be here for him when he needed her. And she knew he would.

She had been through all the nightmares associated with such a loss. Many years ago, she had suffered the same loss as Lucas.

Though she had not lost a life partner, she had lost the love of her life. Robert had been killed in a motorcycle accident, leaving her devastated. After recovering, if a person ever recovers from that, she vowed never to let anyone get close to her again. She never wanted to experience hurt like that again. And she didn't, for years. She went back to college and graduated as a legal secretary. Oh, there were dates of course. After all, there are specific human needs that can be suppressed for only so long. But she managed to keep any relationship at a cool distance. She refused to get involved.

Then came the day she applied for an advertised position with the law firm of Brannigan and Clark. There were very few applicants and she was fortunate to be accepted. She was assigned to the office of Lucas McNab and from that day on, their relationship and respect for each other had grown and developed. She was taken in by Lucas and his wife and the three had shared so many wonderful times together. Gradually Ann had shed her defensive shield and let herself experience life again as she had once known it with Robert. It was as she and Sarah were sisters.

Ann finished her wine and stood up, indicating she was leaving. She was aware that Lucas was not up for any small talk. "Thank you for letting me see you, Lucas. I was deeply concerned about how you were handling everything. Remember, I'm just a phone call away - anytime."

Lucas reached for her empty glass as an excuse to move close to her again. "I really appreciate that, Ann. I'm just now wanting to get out again. I'll remember your offer. Can't tell when I'll be back at the office full time. I'll have to get my mind back on an even keel first. And you might have a part in that, eh?" He helped her on with her coat and had to hold back, aching to hold her close again. He so wanted her to stay with him but did nothing about it. He walked her to the front door, opened it, and placed his hand on her shoulder. As he looked into her eyes he thought he noticed something more than concern. Or was he just imagining something that was missing in his life right now?

"Safe home, Ann, and thanks so much for dropping by. I really appreciate it. See you soon."

"'Nite, Lucas, and just remember what I told you. Anytime."

• • • • •

Breathe next to me and I will capture a piece of your soul with mine.
- Marikit dR. Camba

Ann drove slowly to her apartment, deep in thought. She felt as if she was beginning a long, slow slide into... what? That's what she didn't know. For the present she would be dedicated solely to helping Lucas through his lonely ordeal. 'I just wish I knew the best way to do that,' she mused. Ann pulled up and parked in her driveway, locked the Jeep, and made her way down to her basement apartment. Upon entering, she went to her kitchen, made herself a cup of Red Rose tea, and sat down at her little kitchen table, still deep in thought. She was glad to have made contact with Lucas after these weeks of not knowing how he was doing. She knew quite well what a private person he was and that had kept her away. She remembered referring to his wife Sarah 'understanding'. How could she have been so insensitive! Really. She finished her tea, splashed her face with cold water, and turned in.

Lucas had enjoyed seeing Ann. He had liked holding someone close again, feeling the warmth of her body, breathing in her enticing scent, looking into her beautiful eyes, admiring her perfect body. 'Wait! Don't go there! Their relationship was never about that. Still...' He immediately changed his thinking by pouring himself another scotch. He sat quietly at the kitchen table and slowly the mists of time came rolling in on him like fog. Thoughts of the wonderful years with his wife filled the room with stillness as his eyes filled with tears. 'My God,' he thought, 'it wasn't supposed to end this way. We had years left. We had plans. Our best years were just beginning. Now, here I am alone and I am lost, talking to myself again.' His night ended up like every other night since his wife's passing - in a fitful sleep.

• • • • •

Morning came quite early to Lucas these days. After the usual body flush with strong, dark coffee, he would clean himself up and get ready for the day ahead with little enthusiasm. This day, however, was different. As a result of Ann's short visit last evening he looked forward to this day because he had a plan. He would call Ann before she left for the office and invite her out for breakfast, or at least for coffee. She had said to call her any time, hadn't she? That was the plan. He checked the clock in the kitchen. 7:30. Too early yet. As his mind quieted down, thoughts of his wife appeared. And he felt a twinge of guilt. Guilt about feeling a little happy? Or was it guilt about being happy with another woman? Suddenly the air was escaping from his pretty balloon. Damn, it was a stupid idea anyway. Lucas prepared himself for just another nothing day. Then his phone rang. Who in hell would be calling this early in the morning? He studied the phone for a few seconds, as if he was waiting for it to tell him who it was calling. He picked it up.

"Hello?"

"Good morning, Lucas. Are you up and about yet?" It was Ann's voice on the phone. His plan was back on; Ann had made it happen. He was happy again as thoughts of Sarah slid off into the distance, for now.

"Good morning yourself, Ann. What's this all about?"

"Well, I just thought it might be a good idea for you and me to have coffee together this morning. I called Alison at home and told her what I was doing and to make up some excuse for me. She's a sweetheart and was all for it. So, what do you say?"

"What do I say? I say I'll pick you up in about forty-five minutes. Or do you need more time than that?"

"That's good for me. See you then."

• • • • •

Friendship is a single soul dwelling in two bodies.
- Aristotle

He parked in the street opposite Ann's apartment and gave a short tap on the horn. Watching the side door of the building he saw it open and then Ann emerged into the sunlight. She was dressed in black slacks, white blouse, and a pale tan linen jacket. She had on her familiar quilted red winter coat, not zipped up. She was wearing sunglasses and Lucas thought she looked like a movie star. He got out, opened her door, and watched her manage the rather high step up into the Equinox. Lord, it was good to see her again, so soon. It was quickly becoming obvious to Lucas that Ann was becoming an important part of his emergence.

"Well, now the day is perfect! Ann, thank you so much for your call this morning. You'll never know."

"You are welcome!"

"Okay. Your choice. Where would you like to go?"

"Somewhere quiet. Away from crowds. Do you know of any place like that?"

"I guess that eliminates Timmy's and McDonald's," Lucas said. "Let's just drive and see what we can find. It's Thursday so most people are at their jobs by this time. We should be good."

Lucas drove back into the city maze with its tentacles of streets pulling traffic back and forth. He took Robie Street off of Massachusetts Avenue and turned up Young. He saw the Humani-T

Café coming up on his left and was relieved to see parking in front. There were only a few vehicles and he had no trouble parking.

"What's this place like, Lucas?"

"Well, all I've got to go on is what little information I picked up around the water cooler at the office. Only good reports. I always meant for Sarah and me to come here some time, but we never made it. Willing to give it a go?"

"Absolutely. Lead on, McNab!" Ann gave him a big smile.

They entered the café and were at once astonished with the maze of displays of health-related foods, coffees, teas, and nice little tables spread around. Lucas noticed the curving stairway to the second level and decided that was where they would need to sit to have any privacy. So up they went, to an art gallery with artists' works covering the walls. He took a small table for two against the wall under a lovely painting of a seascape. There was no one else there, and so they had the whole level to themselves. The little waitress came up to take their order. They both decided to try the Canadiana, an organic drip coffee topped up with a shot of espresso.

"Ann. You look absolutely stunning this morning! That's not to say you don't look stunning every morning. Wait... well, you know what I mean, I hope." 'Jeez, what's wrong with me!' he asked himself. 'Wake up and get it together, you idiot!'

"Thank you, Lucas. I know what you're saying. And I'm flattered."

Lucas smiled with relief and thought, 'Okay. Now act your age, you numbskull!'

"Lucas, I had a reason to call you this morning, besides going out for coffee, and I hope I'm doing the right thing. Just remember, I want to help you. What I'm about to talk to you about... well, it's going to be really foreign to you and your thinking. But please, hear me through, and try to keep an open mind. It helped me through my darkest hours after losing Robert, and I'm positive it can help you... or I wouldn't bring it up." She hoped Lucas' feelings for her would allow her leeway to broach the subject.

Lucas studied the evident seriousness in Ann's face, and leaned forward a little, waiting for her to continue. He said nothing.

"Lucas, have you ever heard of the term 'medium'?"

"Yes, I have: it goes right between rare and well done!"

"Please, Lucas, this is rather serious and there's going to be a lot for you to take in."

"Then no, I haven't."

Ann was very apprehensive. In no way did she want to endanger their relationship, but her certainty that a medium could bring a new understanding of life and death to him made her determined to risk that relationship. She must be careful in her approach.

"Lucas, I've told you about Robert and how I was completely devastated. That's how I can understand what you are going through now, losing Sarah. I've been there. I had a good, close friend during that time, Margo, and she explained to me what I want to explain to you now. It probably saved my life, and I'm positive it will help you. But only if you keep an open mind. Will you do that for me? Lucas?"

Lucas was listening intently to what Ann was saying. He sensed that this moment was very important to her, and that made it important to him also.

"Ann, whatever it is you want to tell me... I promise to hear you out and I will try and keep an open mind. Before you start, how's your coffee? Want a refill or anything?"

"Thanks, I'm good. To begin, my friend met me just the same way we're meeting here this morning, and I admit that what she told me, well, it made no sense to me at all. I almost felt insulted. I have no doubt you will most likely feel the same way, maybe even more so. Anyway, here goes."

Ann had piqued Lucas' curiosity. He hadn't seen her so intense before.

"My friend talked to me about..." 'Oh God, this is it!' She was afraid of how Lucas would react. Would it all end here, or would she be able to go on "...an... afterlife." She studied his face for any reaction to what she had just said. She thought she could see a questioning in

R . B .   B r o w n

his eyes. Lucas was still listening and Ann understood that she could continue. She gave a deep sigh and continued.

"I know pretty much what you're thinking, Lucas, but I'll explain as best I can. The next thing Margo said was that we all have a soul or spirit, if you like, that is made up of energy. She explained that when our body dies, our spirit, our soul, leaves the body and ascends to another existence, another plane where we live again." 'Lord,' Ann thought, 'if I was hearing this for the first time I would think I was losing my mind. It does sound radical.' Her eyes never left Lucas' eyes, holding them in an unblinking stare. His attitude never altered. She went on.

"She talked to me about mediums and what they are able to do. She explained how they can communicate with souls that have passed. She was as serious as I am now. She let me digest all of what she just told me, and I'll admit, I had a lot of trouble making sense of it all. But she eventually got me to visit a reputable medium that she knew, and I was reluctant - *very* reluctant, let me tell you. However, I went with her. I pictured an old woman in a darkened room wearing a turban and cloak, a glass globe before her on a table, a black cat sitting on her lap. This was a picture in my mind of what I had learned about mysticism growing up, but it was nothing like that at all. She was a well-dressed lady, perhaps in her late forties, living in a very nice house in Beechville. She had a degree in psychology from Dal. Quite ordinary, really."

Ann watched Lucas' face carefully. Nothing out of the ordinary that she could see ... yet.

"She explained to me what would be taking place, that whatever spirit came through, it would say or ask something to let me know who it was, something that only I would know. It was the spirit's way of letting me know that the spirit was exactly who it claimed to be. I had planned to take notes, but Margo said she would do that for me so that I could concentrate on who was coming through. And she began. My mother came through first and by statements and questions she quickly verified it was her. Then Robert came through, and from what he said it was definitely him! The medium said things that only Robert and myself knew. His identification was absolute. The medium would have had no idea of certain situations or phrases used between us. The reading, that's what the sessions are called, went on for about forty-five minutes. I was in complete shock!

"Later, when Margo and I went back over her notes, I was even more astounded by what had come through. It became so obvious to me that there had to be another plane, that we absolutely have a soul which does not die as the body does. Lucas, I can't tell you what a comfort that knowledge was to me at that time. The experience showed me that Robert's spirit was alive and still with me. I just was unable to make contact like the medium could. That first reading completely changed my life. My grief gradually left me and I was a changed person for the better. Over the years I 'talked' with Robert many times, when I needed solace."

There. It was all out in the open. Ann released a long, audible sigh and lowered her eyes to her now cold cup of coffee. She didn't dare look at Lucas for what seemed like several minutes, but it was only a few long seconds. When she did raise her head, Lucas was still looking at her, but his face was different. What was it? Questioning? Anger? Disbelief? She couldn't read his expression. Ann reached across the small table for his hand and he pulled back a little, his eyes still fixated on her face. 'Oh Lord, what have I done?' she asked herself.

Lucas had listened intently to every word Ann had said, not making judgement on any aspect of her story. But the more she said, the more he found it improbable, like the ramblings of the demented. Why was she telling him all this… Why was she assaulting his Christian beliefs that had been imbedded in his brain since childhood? He was truly stunned by her revelations.

"That's quite a story, Ann. Is there a point, anywhere?"

What could she say? She didn't dare tell him her reason for the story. That would have been too much for him to accept all at one time.

"It was just an experience I had, sort of out of the ordinary, that had a profound, a *very* profound effect on my life at a time when I needed it. Don't dismiss it out of hand, Lucas. And please, don't think I need to see a shrink or anything like that." Ann was regretting her decision. Was it too soon? Probably... too soon. "Forget about the whole thing, Lucas. It's just an experience I had," she repeated. Ann hoped this change in her attitude might affect Lucas in the right way; she hoped that he might think about her experience more when he was alone. Or would it queer their relationship forever? Time. He would need time.

They left the café and Lucas drove Ann back to her apartment. Neither spoke during the trip. Lucas parked in the same place he had parked earlier, reached across Ann, and opened the door. Ann undid her seatbelt, stepped out, turned to him and said simply, "Call me." Lucas looked into those beautiful eyes and nodded his head.

• • • • •

Don't tell them too much about your soul. They're waiting for that.
- Jack Kerouac

Lucas' thoughts were confused as he made the trip back to the house on Gateway. What had happened, all of a sudden? The morning had started out so well. Ann looked great and he had actually felt better than he had in a long time. He really was puzzled over what Ann had talked about. What *had* she talked about? She had mentioned Robert and something about feelings. And what the hell is a medium?

He parked in the driveway, not really wanting to see the Miata again, and went in through the front door. He checked the time. 10:20. Jeez, that didn't last long. He supposed he could have... should have made a day out of it, but Ann had put a damper on the morning with her nonsense, so he thought. He made himself a single cup of coffee with a coffee press and took it out to the sunroom, which was still in the morning shade. Lucas looked longingly at his wife's picture and couldn't stop the sadness he felt welling up inside. My God, it hurt so much. Grief was the only constant in his life. It was always there, just under the surface, waiting to hurt him again. 'Sarah, Sarah, Sarah! I miss you so much. You've left me all alone. I love you so much. I know I could have done more for you, but I did my best, sweetheart. You were in so much pain at the end.' Tears coursed down his tired face as he saw her as she used to be, happy and… alive. She had taken all the good with her. He sat in the leather chair where they had always sat together with their coffees to start the day. They had talked about anything, as long as they liked.

Sarah's dementia had started slowly, in a quiet, evil way. Other people had noticed it long before Lucas did. Any great differences he had picked up on were simply an age thing, or so he thought. It happened to everybody. But then something else took hold of Sarah's body. She became unsteady and unable to take her walks she dearly loved. And reached a point where Lucas had to help her up out of bed. And he made the meals and fed her as he watched her fade farther and farther away from him. She became quite helpless near the end. Hospice care came in regularly and looked after her toilet. Lucas and Sarah had made a pact years ago. Neither one would ever go to a home of any kind or to a hospital. In truth, they had been sincere when they had promised they would go together. Lucas discovered how cheap talk was. Sarah's condition didn't even allow him to think about that promise. Then one evening Sarah went into a coma. Lucas was beside Sarah as she took her last breath. He stayed with her, running his hand back and forth across her forehead for a very long time before calling 911.

Lucas kept reliving those last days, vividly, like they had happened yesterday - they were that clear in his mind. 'Oh Sarah, I should have done so much more. Forgive me, my love.' He closed his eyes and tried to close his mind to his troublesome thoughts. He sat for a short while, then bolted upright in the chair, spilling what little coffee was left in his cup.

'What the...' Lucas' eyes widened in disbelief. What had he just done? He had talked to Sarah! She hadn't answered him, but he had just talked to his wife. He had talked to her a few times over the last few weeks, and he had never realized it. 'I'll be damned,' he thought, amazed at what had just taken place.

Then he remembered Ann's conversation at the café, and it slowly came into focus. It started to make sense. He sat back in the chair and studied his wife's picture again. She was smiling as if to say, 'Now you're getting it!'

• • • • •

Lucas didn't call Ann immediately. He wanted to, of course, but first he wanted to think about all that had happened this morning. He wanted to try and form some sort of understanding of what Ann had laid out at the café. After all, he wasn't a stupid man. This wasn't like solving a murder case or anything like that. But then again...

'Let's see now. Ann had talked about another plane, a higher level of something where the soul goes. She also called it your spirit. And your soul or spirit lives on after death. I think that's how she put it. The soul leaves your body after you die. Hmmmm. That all seems highly implausible, right now. Wait now, is that what the Bible means when it tells about going up to heaven?' He recalled, 'In my father's house is many rooms, or something like that. So what happens after you get to this other... place?' He was quickly approaching the conclusion that he wanted to know more. He wanted to know all of it.

"Hello?" Ann answered the phone in a quizzical tone.

"Hi, Ann. It's me. Lucas."

"Well, this is sooner than I expected." She sensed an excitement in his voice. "What do you want?"

"Can I come over? Am I interrupting anything?"

"No, no. That's fine. Come on over. Have you eaten yet?"

"No, I haven't eaten at all," Lucas realized.

"Good. We'll have something here. See you soon."

Ann ended the call and smiled. She was relieved that things between them seemed to be back to normal. She went about putting together some cheese and crackers along with some rolled up slices of peppercorn turkey, and then she dressed the plate up with some sweet gherkins. 'That should do it,' she thought. 'Lucas is a picker anyway. A cup of tea might be good, too.' But she would wait to check on that. It wasn't long until she heard the light rapping on her door.

"It's open."

Lucas came in carrying a Bible in one hand and a legal writing pad in the other.

"Hi, Ann. I apologize about this morning at the café. I was way out of line. I understand now what you were trying to do. And I get it, I think."

"No apology necessary. It's just good to see you. What have you got there?" Ann motioned to the Bible and notebook.

"Tools of the trade, I hope."

Lucas set his 'tools' on the little kitchen table and sat down on one of the two chairs. Ann picked up the plate she had prepared plate and set it in the middle of the table. Then she sat down opposite him.

His eyes took a quick sweep around her tiny compact living space. He was surprised to realize he had never been inside Ann's apartment.

"Now, Lucas, tell me what this is all about."

Now it was his turn to take a deep breath. He looked intently at Ann. "This is quite a turnaround for me, but I just realized, today, after I dropped you off, that I've been talking to Sarah almost since the day she… and all the time I thought I was just talking to myself! You see what I'm saying?"

Ann wanted to climb over the table and give Lucas the biggest hug ever! "Oh, Lucas, I am so pleased you came to this realization." Instead, she gave herself a hug, and pretended. "Oh, that is so good!"

"Well, Ann, I want to tell you that our conversation, rather *your* conversation, at the café stuck with me more than I knew. The realization hit me like a thunderbolt! And the more I thought about everything, the more I came around to the idea of a medium. I think I'm open to doing that now." He stood up, pushed back the chair, walked around to her, held out his arms, and smiled. Ann did the same and their hug was warm and loving. Nothing would ever be the same between them.

Ann was excited for herself and Lucas over the prospect of having him experience contact with the 'other side'. She just knew it would shock him, in a good, positive way. The best part was that he had arrived at his decision on his own. That was so important to someone like Lucas. Ann didn't care how it happened, just that it happened! She mentioned that perhaps it would be good to contact the medium she knew and had visited a few times. 'It would make it easier for all,' she reasoned.

Working from that premise, the next morning Ann called the medium she knew and trusted, Rosalie Francoeur. Explaining that she had a dear friend who could benefit greatly from a reading, she managed to obtain an appointment only two days away. Ann hoped that Lucas wouldn't develop 'cold feet' in the interim. She would keep her fingers crossed just the same. She called Lucas to let him know about the appointment. She could prepare him for the experience later on.

When Lucas returned home from Ann's, he felt pleased with his decision to see a medium. And he knew he was fortunate to have Ann be his guide through these uncharted waters. He was anxious. Two days. What could he do to occupy himself for two days? What about the computer? He might find something there on mediums that might prepare him a bit.

After pressing a cup of strong coffee, he sat down in front of his computer, an older desktop that was a bit temperamental but served his few trips into never never land. He punched in 'medium'. He would laugh if he was directed to sites about the cooking of steak, thinking back to the morning at the Humani-T café.

Not finding anything that related to what he was looking for, he scrolled down and found 'People also ask'. There were two questions: What is **medium**, which he ignored; and What is a **medium** or **media**. He leaned in to the screen as he read:

> '*Media is used in reference to mass communication such as newspapers, radio, the internet, and so on. It's also used in science where* **medium** *usually means an intervening substance through which something is transmitted.* **Mediums** *is the plural when* **medium** *refers to a person who...* **communicates with... the dead!**'

Lucas involuntarily sat back in his chair. That was the word he had so much trouble saying. There it was... being used in the same breath as *medium*! Seeing it in print like this made it seem macabre! He quickly turned off the computer and took a big swallow of coffee. The definition on the screen had seemed so stark and harsh, not like Ann's definition at all. Which was right? Both! But he hoped fervently that Ann's was the one he would be working from. He took his coffee and went into the living room, hoping that some TV drivel would drive out of his mind what he had just read. It didn't. 'Two days,' he thought. 'Can I keep my resolve for two days?' If he decided against this whole medium thing, he knew how disappointed Ann would be. After all, she was doing it to help him out of his despair. 'Buck up,' he told himself, 'you have to give it a chance.' Without knowing why, he opted out of having a scotch before turning in. He felt he had to keep his mind clear. He thought it might have something to do with Ann coming back into his life. She definitely had an effect on him in a positive way, and he felt good about it. Just her presence picked him up.

• • • • •

The following morning Lucas decided it might be a good idea to do a bit of house cleaning. He had let everything in that line 'go to the dogs', and now it just had to be done. After all, there was a woman in his life again. Not a Sarah, but a good friend. 'And Ann was right,' he admitted. 'Sarah would have been okay with me going out with Ann.' Then he realized that they hadn't been on what you might call a date yet. There was always an underlying reason to meet. 'Perhaps that's just as well,' he rationalized.

He took out the little Shark vacuum cleaner and vacuumed all the floors on the first level of the house. 'They do look better,' he thought. Dusting was something else. He usually avoided looking for dust and therefore never saw the need *to* dust. Now, he saw it everywhere. He got the Swiffer duster Sarah had purchased, as well as numerous other Swiffer products she had thought would make house cleaning easier. Lucas had cleaned sporadically while looking after Sarah. He wasn't too careful with his dusting, but just got it done. When he had finished all he was prepared to do that day, he made a bold decision. He would investigate hiring someone to clean the house. That was that.

Lucas killed more time by doing grocery shopping. 'You can waste a lot of time grocery shopping,' he told himself. He felt fortunate in not encountering anyone he knew and having to endure condolences which just set him back into despair. All in all, it wasn't too bad an experience. Each time he had to undertake tasks, like grocery shopping, he compared it to taking another step toward learning to walk again. He had done all of these tasks before while taking care of his wife, certainly, but now there was a whole different purpose. Now he did it for him alone, and the shopping list had changed, as had everything else in his life.

He had purposely left his watch at home just so he wouldn't be looking at it continuously. Now he wished he had worn it. What was the time, anyway? It must be getting late. The sky was overcast with the fading light. He could tell the temperature was dropping. It was going to be a cold night. Entering the Equinox, he checked the time on the dash: 5:05. He wondered what Ann was doing. He might give her a call later on just to see how she was making out. Oops! A Freudian slip? Wishful thinking, maybe? He smiled to himself and immediately felt guilty of betraying his wife. He had to stop that thinking.

He put the Chev in the garage when he got home, not sure what odd weather the night might bring. He cast a quick glimpse at the Miata, and then he brought what few groceries he had purchased into the house. He had just taken his coat off when the phone rang. He hoped it was Ann.

"Hello?"

"Hi, Lucas." It was her.

"Hi Ann. I just got in. Went grocery shopping."

"I knew you were out. I tried calling several times."

"Just putting in time, Ann. Keeping busy. Watching the hours creep slowly by."

"I know, I know. Just one more day. Listen, since I know where we have to go, I'll take my Jeep and I'll drive. Is that all right with you?"

"That makes sense. What time did you say the appointment was?" Lucas grabbed a pencil and note pad.

"Three o'clock. We should leave your place about two, or shortly after."

"I'm looking forward to the experience, Ann. See you then. Take care."

• • • • •

When the appointed day finally arrived, Lucas was up early, show-ered and dressed for the cold front which had been forecasted to hit the province later that night. Good warm socks for his winter boots, jeans, white t-shirt, and a blue plaid outer shirt. Best to be prepared, he thought, knowing how changeable the Maritime weather could be.

In the kitchen he opted for a couple of scrambled eggs with a slice of ham, toast, and coffee. Usually that big of a breakfast would do him for most of the day. But today, he could have eaten it all over again. It must be the excitement plus a little nervousness making him hungrier than usual. He paced around the house, watched some news on TV, turned the radio on, then off. He watched the morning through the picture window in the living room. Looking at the blue sky he saw two planes almost side by side, laying down the familiar chem trails. He had ignored his interest in geoengineering for a long time since his wife had required his full attention. 'I'll have to get back to those bastards one of these days,' he thought.

The time crept slowly by for Lucas. He opened the fridge to see if there was anything that might make a sandwich, not that he was hungry, but he might be before Ann showed up. Nothing registered, and so he closed the door. He picked out his down-filled parka, found his scarf and gloves, and placed everything on a kitchen chair. He checked the outdoor thermometer for the temperature. Minus five Fahrenheit. He had kept the old thermometer after Trudeau had brought in Celsius because he just couldn't buy into the reasoning for the change. He still calculated in inches too.

Ann arrived sometime after two o'clock and noticed at once that Lucas was slightly agitated. She wasn't overly surprised. This would be a monumental step for him. If he accepted what he experienced today, she knew it would be life-altering for him.

"Hope you dressed warmly enough, Ann. Did you hear the forecast for tonight?"

"Yes, I dressed for the weather, Lucas. Don't you worry. You ready to go?"

"Ready, I guess I am. Let's get going, girl!"

The left the house and climbed into Ann's Compass Trailhawk. It was still cozy warm from the drive.

"You know, Ann, I could never figure out what possessed you to get such an ungodly colour as this orange-red, or red-orange, and then top it off with a black roof! What were you thinking?"

"Well, at the time I believed I was making a statement about something. And now I never worry about not being able to find it in a parking lot!" Ann smiled smugly across the roof of the Jeep at Lucas, and he smiled back, winking in acknowledgement.

Ann backed the Jeep out of the driveway on to Gateway, followed the road down to the Bedford Highway, and turned right, ahead of traffic, heading into the city. She then took Joseph Howe Drive to the traffic circle or roundabout and turned on to number three, St. Margaret's Bay Road. Ann noticed that Lucas appeared deep in thought so she left him alone and concentrated on driving. The traffic wasn't all that bad for a Monday. Of course, at this time of day the working traffic was still parked.

She took the short Lighthouse Route turn off which put her on Prospect Road. It had been a while since she had made this trip to see Rosalie. After their initial contact, Ann had done only phone readings. She hoped she remembered how to find her. She passed the Chain Lakes and drove along a stretch of woods, past the Exhibition Centre, then the Goodwood Family Golf Centre with driving range and mini putt.

Lucas sat up and took notice of his surroundings. He couldn't remember ever having been to this part of the country. It was quite built up. 'A bedroom community,' he supposed. 'Ah, that's Dow and Duggan Log Homes.'

"Ann, what in the world got you out this way? I know it's where the medium is, but surely there must be mediums in the city."

"Sure there are. But my friend, Margo, had been to Rosalie several times and found her to be excellent. You know, Lucas, locating a medium that you like and trust is a lot like buying a used car. If you don't have advice from previous 'owners' you take a chance. It's just that way with choosing a medium. And keep in mind that after your reading today it can be done by phone, which I really like."

"Why is that?"

"It's more relaxed, and you don't have this drive!"

"So you don't have to be in person?"

"Absolutely not. Some people, on recommendation, only do phone readings. I've found them absolutely as accurate. Mind you, there are charlatans in this business as you might suspect. This is why we make this trip today. Rosalie is the real deal. She's proven herself, time and time again. It's a gift, Lucas. And the true mediums are amazing. They haven't asked for the ability to do this sort of thing. Some apparently are born with it. It happens to others after some life-altering experience. One thing not to do is volunteer any information. Rosalie wouldn't appreciate that at all!"

Lucas saw how built up it was, all along the road. Nice, well-kept properties, little Nova Scotia bungalows, as they were called. His house wasn't much larger, he guessed. They were now following large bodies of water; this was beautiful scenery. He checked the dash clock. It read 2:40. Ann was making good time, adhering to the 'suggested' speed limits. He couldn't help but wonder what effect a blizzard would have on these roads. Surely it would take some time before they were plowed out. He marvelled at the closeness of the shoulder of the road to the water's edge in some places, picturing a storm surge and huge waves billowing over the pavement. He gave a slight shudder at the thought of such a storm. The water in the cove they were driving past showed that cold looking blue-grey colour with small white caps forming. 'A person wouldn't last very long in that water,' he thought.

• • • • •

"Ah, here's the village, finally." Ann's voice showed some relief in having found it again. "I remember her house was a light blue, I think. Let's hope she hasn't painted it since the last time I was here." Ann was intently searching through the cluster of little houses on the rocky peninsula. "Hey, there it is! Just as I remember it." Ann parked in front of the little blue 'salt-box' New England-style house. They both left the Jeep and Ann walked up to the brick-red, windowless front door and knocked.

While they waited for a response, Lucas eyed the darkening sky and figured the storm would likely arrive sooner than it had been forecast. He looked over the small cluster of houses, thinking that cottages would be a more apt description for most. The village gave the impression of buildings that might have crawled out of the sea and grabbed a foothold on the rough, rocky ground and held on for dear life.

"Not too many basements, I'll venture," Lucas commented to himself.

Little wharves were scattered here and there, jutting out to the sea. Some looked pretty rickety, Lucas noticed. Over there was a large red building. Storage and baiting? Probably. Looking seaward, he saw several islands, and thought this would be a really enjoyable place for kayaking.

After a short wait the door opened, with some difficulty, and a little lady appeared. Rosalie smiled and took Ann's proffered hand with both of hers.

"Come in, come in, my dear. It's turning quite cold out and we have some weather coming in too!"

Lucas entered the house behind Ann and was introduced to Rosalie.

"Rosalie, this is Lucas McNab. I set up this appointment for him. I hope that's all right."

"Of course it's all right, child." Rosalie reached for Lucas' hand. "How do you do, Mr. McNab? I'm very pleased to meet you. Will this be your first time having a reading?"

"Pleased to meet you. Yes, this is my first time. Be gentle." Lucas smiled at his little joke but Rosalie paid no attention. Ann, on the other hand, frowned at Lucas as if to say, 'Be serious', and from that moment on, he was.

Rosalie led them into the small dining room, its walls covered with framed pictures of people from various periods of history as well as friends and relatives, Lucas surmised. All photos were black and white, or sepia. Rosalie saw Lucas looking at the collection. "That larger picture, Mr. McNab, is of my husband. He passed fifteen years ago. He was a fisherman, as nearly all the men are, or were. Not much fishing taking place now. Big companies pretty much control everything now." Lucas looked more closely at the picture of Rosalie's husband. A rugged face, shaped by the sea. A hard life evident. 'Fifteen years,' he thought. 'That's a long time living alone. Especially way out here.'

"You can sit here, Mr. McNab." Rosalie indicated an older straight-backed wooden chair.

"Thank you, Rosalie. May I call you Rosalie? It's a beautiful name. You can call me Lucas."

"That'll be fine, Mr. McNab... Lucas."

"I'll sit back here and take notes for Lucas if I may, Rosalie." Ann sat on a lightly upholstered armchair, in front of the little front window, a clipboard resting on her lap.

"Certainly, child. You do just that. That will be fine."

Rosalie sat down opposite Lucas, in an identical chair to his. She carefully moved a small green glass vase with artificial flowers to the side of the table.

"Well now, shall we begin?" The old lady looked intently at Lucas. "Please understand, Mr... Lucas, that I have no control over who decides to come across. It might be someone you would least expect.

Also, the person contacted might present information, questions perhaps, that have no bearing on what you are searching for. It will just be their way of proving to you who they are."

Ann, with her pencil poised over a blank sheet of paper, watched Lucas closely. She leaned in toward the table, making sure she could hear everything Rosalie would be saying.

Lucas, feeling a bit nervous and apprehensive, never took his eyes off of Rosalie's face. In fact, he was quite nervous. This was worse than a courtroom. There he had control to a large degree. Here, his control was gone. All control was in the hands of this older lady. A whole new experience for him.

Rosalie closed her eyes and tilted her head back slightly. She stayed like that for a few seconds. Lucas thought, 'That's effective' and wondered if *was* just for effect.

Then Rosalie looked directly at Lucas and said, "I see much stress around you. Sadness. You have a lot of sadness. I sense a lot of tears around you. I see a man and a woman coming forward. Do you know a Mac or Malcolm? He is here to support you."

Malcolm was Lucas' father! "My father," was all Lucas could utter.

"You feel adrift right now. I'm looking at a boat in very rough water. Your father is keeping you safe. He's holding the boat with ropes. There is another man. He is older. He is related to your father. He is here to help you too. He is helping your father."

'Grandfather?' wondered Lucas.

"There is an older woman. Do you recognize the name Janet? Or Jessie? She is with the men. She says she is your mother. She says not to worry... that everyone there has your back."

Everything was going so fast that Lucas had little time to take in fully what Rosalie was telling him. He prayed that Ann was recording everything Rosalie was saying.

Rosalie continued. "You have to let go of any guilt you are feeling. You have nothing to feel guilty about. Your father says he was a very good forty-fives player. He says always play the person, not the cards.

He's proud he never cheated. He says you have a much better hand than you think, but someone is dealing from the bottom of the deck.

"Your mother says there is a heaviness in your heart. She comes to comfort you. A name comes through from the spirit world. Charles or Chuck. Do these names mean anything to you? The name is all I have."

Lucas shook his head.

After a pause, Rosalie looked at Lucas and continued. "January was a very difficult month for you. Very sensitive for you. And in November and December you felt you had lost control of everything. Is that right?"

Again, Lucas simply nodded his head in the affirmative. Then Rosalie added, "I don't see much stability in your life until much later this year. And I see a major change in your career happening. Late spring, possibly."

Lucas was completely enthralled with all that Rosalie had said. Again, he prayed Ann was taking good notes. Where was his wife? Where was his Sarah? Why hadn't she come through? He decided to give Rosalie another focus without prompting her.

"Rosalie, I would like to talk with a lady named Sarah."

"I have her here. She has been standing off, watching how this is done. Her passing was very emotional. Unexpected, perhaps? She says it wasn't easy to let go. She says she would come back in a heartbeat if it wasn't for the pain. Do you understand this, Lucas?"

Lucas gulped back a tear and nodded.

"Okay. She says for you to be happy. Don't keep thinking about the sad things in life. She is laughing. She loves the sound of laughter. She still loves to read. She shows me lots of books. She says she wasn't afraid, and that you lost her twice. She says she didn't want to become a vegetable. She didn't want a long, drawn out experience. She says she loved the sound of your voice. She laughs and says that you never shut up.

"Sarah is very happy. She likes music very much. I see her playing a grand piano. Classical. She says you don't have to be brave. And don't put anything off. Take trips. You and she will be together and she won't cost you anything. She laughs.

"She is around you all the time. She likes to hold your hand. One of your hands will feel different from the other. That will be Sarah holding that hand.

"She says she will bring another lady into your life as she doesn't want you to be alone. But she adds that you are to remember that you still belong to her!

"They are all leaving now. Just know they all love you and are protecting you."

Lucas was in awe of what he had just been a part of. He felt exhausted from the concentration required to follow what had unfolded. The information from Rosalie was fast and precise. Ann's notes were going to be very important. He took Rosalie's hand in both of his.

"Rosalie, thank you so much for the reading, and for taking me on such short notice. It was an experience. I appreciate it. Thank you. You have been most gracious."

Rosalie held his hand for several seconds, looking Lucas full in the face, studying him. She made Lucas a bit uncomfortable. "You are very welcome, Mr. McNab. I believe I will see you again."

Lucas pushed back the chair and eased away from the table. He finally looked at Ann who was positively beaming. She rose from the armchair and reached over to simply touch his arm. He gave her a warm look of appreciation. Rosalie followed them out to the little hall entrance. Lucas asked what she charged and payed her. He was about to ask for her telephone number and then quickly realized that Ann would have it.

They said their goodbyes and opened the front door. They saw that the snow had already started. They gave a final wave to Rosalie who was still standing in the doorway waving.

Lucas asked Ann if she would like him to drive, but she said she was perfectly capable. Knowing that she was, he climbed into the passenger's side.

• • • • •

The short drive back to the city took considerably longer because of the snow, or what passed as snow, which was coming down heavier by the minute. What traffic was on the road was driving very carefully and Ann fell in line, thankful for her all-wheel drive.

Several minutes passed with both of them silent, Ann straining to keep the Jeep in the tracks of the cars ahead. She didn't want to interrupt whatever thoughts Lucas might be having. The Jeep's windshield wipers were having increasing difficulty in removing the snow that kept plastering on the windshield. Visibility was getting worse. They probably had another seven or eight miles to go to the city. Ann couldn't tell exactly where they were, so that was just a guess. The strain of the drive demanded her full concentration and kept them both quiet.

Eventually they drove closer to the city surrounds with more light to penetrate the curtain of snow. Ann entered the roundabout. She barely found the turn off to Joseph Howe Drive, but once on it, she was able to relax. They would soon be home.

Traffic on the Bedford Highway was quite heavy but drivers were being cautious. The dash clock showed 5:03 and there wasn't much daylight left. In fact, there was hardly any.

"Lucas, come to my place tonight. I've got room and I'll take you back tomorrow. Lots of food. No scotch but some wine. I know you'd love a scotch right about now. What do you say? Tell me quickly, your turn off is coming right up."

Ann was right. He would love a scotch, or two. But wine would do.

"Your place it is." Lucas wanted to talk about his reading and Ann's basement apartment seemed the perfect place.

A short while later she made the left turn onto Torrington Drive in Sherwood Heights, turned off Torrington onto Lynwood Drive, slowed down, and drove up a wide driveway to the two-storey brick bungalow. She parked the Jeep beside a small black sedan.

Ann opened the door of the Jeep, jumped down into the snow that was now a good six inches deep, and ran to the roofed side entrance of the house. Lucas was right on her heels. Ann had her key in her hand and was trying to insert it into the deadbolt keyway. She clumsily dropped it in the snow at her feet. Lucas quickly found it and finished unlocking the door. They stepped into the dark entryway where Ann found the light switch, and then they carefully made their way down a flight of stairs. Ann opened this second door, stepped inside, and disappeared in the dark. She soon turned on a light.

Lucas stepped into a beautifully laid out kitchen and dining area. Though it was a bit small, it was perfect for one person. He wondered why he had never taken more notice the interior previously.

"Ann, this is a great kitchen."

Lucas saw that it had everything a kitchen required. 'Not much counter space, but enough for Ann,' he imagined. Three small cupboards and drawers and doors under the counter would have held everything that was needed to make it complete. Lucas noticed the small sink set at the end of the counter against the wall. That would have bothered him had he lived here. There was a little drop-leaf table and two chairs and the table had a Nova Scotia tartan tablecloth.

"Come see the rest of it, Lucas. In here is my living room, and a hide-a-bed for company, which is you tonight. Recliner rocker, hassock, bookcase, TV and stand. What more could I need?"

"What more indeed! It's truly very cozy."

Lucas saw a few art posters on the walls. He couldn't tell right off who had done the originals, but he sensed that they were well done. He saw a few framed coloured pictures, of family, Lucas surmised. 'Wait, what was that one over by the TV?' Lucas took a few steps to get closer. The people looked familiar, and they should have. It was the three of them: Ann, Sarah, and him. That brought back some memories. He wasn't able to place where the photo had been taken. Not much background was showing but he thought it might have been taken not too long before he lost Sarah. She looked a bit pale and had begun to lose weight. 'We all look pretty cheerful,' he thought.

Ann stepped out of her bedroom, having towelled off somewhat. "The bathroom is just through here," she said, gesturing behind herself to her bedroom.

"Thanks. I could use some drying off, for sure." Lucas stepped into what turned out to be Ann's bedroom, and he immediately felt uneasy, like he shouldn't be in her *bedroom*! He quickly grabbed the towel Ann had set out for him, and then he walked quickly back to the living room. He had felt like he should have covered his eyes in there. How silly was that!

He smelled the delicious aroma of fresh brewing coffee. Lucas continued drying his hair, patting it down to some semblance of normalcy. 'What to do with the towel?' He looked at the bedroom. 'Nope. Not back in there.' He decided to take it with him to the kitchen. There would be someplace there to put it.

"You smelled the coffee, huh. I've got white wine if you'd rather."

"That coffee smells perfect for a winter's night like this. Coffee it is. Hey, that sounds like it could be a Lightfoot song, doesn't it? Ann, do you have your notes from the reading?"

"Sure do. Let's sit down here at the table, okay? Get a couple of mugs from the cupboard and pour. Milk's in the fridge. Spoons in the drawer to the left. I'll get my notes."

Lucas suddenly realized he felt more comfortable here, in Ann's tiny apartment, then he had felt in his own house in weeks. That surprised him, but he let it pass. He put the two mugs of coffee on the table and arranged the two chairs side by side, not too close together, as Ann came back with her clipboard.

They both pulled the chairs out from the table and sat down, slightly nudging each other in the process, and each mumbling 'sorry'. Ann unclipped her notes and spread them out in order. She picked up the first one, then put it back down. She turned and looked at Lucas, who turned and met her stare.

"Now, tell me, Lucas, and be honest. What's your overall impression of what took place today?"

"Right. Honest. Ann, I'm not sure what took place with Rosalie today. It's a lot to take in, especially for a dyed-in-the-wool skeptic like me. I believe Rosalie is honest and well-intentioned, but seeing and talking to dead people, I don't understand how that is possible. I am just horribly confused right now. That's all I can say. Maybe the lawyer in me makes me this way. I don't know, Ann."

"Okay, Lucas. Let's take it one step at a time then." Ann picked up the first page of her notes. "The sadness. Think. Sure, she could have read that in your face, your demeanour. I'll give you that. But what about naming your father? How could that happen? Does she read minds? You weren't even thinking about your father, were you? And she got the name right off."

Lucas was watching Ann but his mind was back at Rosalie's. He slowly nodded his head, not making any comment.

"All right. Did your father play forty-fives? Was he a good player like he claimed?"

"Good Lord, Ann. Who in Nova Scotia *didn't* play forty-fives? Yes, he loved to play, and yes, he was a good player, but cheat? You bet he cheated. I can remember he and Uncle Eddie and Mom's sister, Bertha, would visit and they would set up to play - men against the women. Well, Aunt Bertha would get so mad at Dad and Eddie, she would pitch the cards on the floor and stomp out of the room. Yes, he cheated, but it was all in fun. He was very competitive and hated to lose."

"Well, she was only repeating what the spirit of your father was telling her. She did get the card game right. Let's see now." Ann used her finger to follow down the page of scribbled notes. "You say you don't know a Charles or a Chuck."

"That's right."

"Well, keep the name in mind and don't be surprised if he shows up somewhere down the line. She was correct with the months and how you were affected at that time, wasn't she?"

Again, Lucas just nodded his head in response.

"Lucas, her descriptions regarding your feelings were spot on, I think."

He answered Ann this time. "Well, those were all-encompassing and could cover a large range of situations a person might be going through. Right?"

Ann didn't answer. She sensed that he did not believe much of what had taken place at Rosalie's.

"Lucas, keep in mind that mediums not only contact those souls that have crossed over, but they also read the person in front of them too. Yes, the reading is all-encompassing. In that sense, the medium is also a psychic. It's just part of the whole."

Psychic! As if he wasn't confused enough! Now Ann brings this into the picture. He leaned back in his chair and thoughtfully drank the rest of his coffee.

"Would you like a refill?"

"No thanks, Ann, but I would appreciate a glass of your wine. The coffee's not doing it for me anymore. My head is spinning with all of this!"

Ann got up, opened one of the doors under the counter, and then came up with a bottle of South African Riesling. Taking two large wine glasses from the top cabinet, she carefully poured a good measure into each glass. It was just cold enough under the counter to suit the wine. Lucas took a large mouthful and let it warm up a bit in his mouth before swallowing.

"Oh, that is good, Ann. Thank you," he said, as he again leaned back in his chair.

"It's more comfortable in the living room. Want to move in there?"

"Later. I want to do more on this reading. I want to try to understand what Rosalie said about Sarah first. Can we do that? Besides, I want to keep the wine close." Lucas smiled at Ann to let her know everything was all right.

Suddenly, Ann realized they hadn't eaten anything since lunch, and maybe Lucas hadn't even had that!

"Lucas! You must be starving, dear man. Come to think of it, I am too. I'll scare up something for us."

"Since you mentioned it, I do feel a bit peckish. Can I help at all?"

"Sure can. See if you can find the cheese in the fridge. There should be some shaved roast beef in there too. And mayo. On the door will be some horseradish and honey mustard. Got all that?"

"Wait, I'm writing it all down," he joked. Lucas opened the fridge door, surveyed the contents quickly, and managed to locate all items except the mayo.

"Can't seem to find the mayo, Ann. Sure it's here?"

"Never mind. We don't need it. There might be some olives on the door rack. Want to check? Oh, and butter."

Ann was busy cutting thick slices of crusty white bread. Lucas laid everything she had requested on the little counter. It barely held everything. When the sandwiches were ready she brought a plateful to the table.

"Ummm, those smell wonderful. Thank you so much."

"You're welcome. I apologize for being such a poor hostess, but I got caught up in the reading."

"Hey, don't apologize! I'm enjoying the evening. It was an excellent idea, coming over here. I think I needed a break from my too familiar surroundings."

Ann thought to herself, 'Yes, it was a brilliant idea.' When she had made the offer to him in the Jeep, she wasn't sure just how he would take it. He was so silent on the trip back she had wondered about his state of mind.

"You know, if I am to believe all that Rosalie said, I wonder about that change in work for me. Can you find that in your notes? I'd like to read that part."

Ann put her half-eaten sandwich back on the plate and leafed through her notes.

"Here it is. She mentioned a career change, possibly in late spring."

Lucas was just finishing his sandwich. The wine followed.

"Aha. Career change. What else am I good at? Late spring. We shall see, eh?"

Ann finished eating. She cleared the table, pouring more wine before she removed the bottle. As she sat back down at the table, Lucas looked through her notes.

"Can't find your notes on Sarah," Lucas said.

"Just wait. I'll find them." Ann shuffled the papers around and found the notes Lucas was looking for.

"Here you go. Want me to read them?"

"Yes, please. I can follow better by listening."

Ann carefully and deliberately read all the information Rosalie had provided regarding Sarah. A fair amount of information had been given to Rosalie. Ann paused after each comment, allowing Lucas to take it all in.

He sat, head bowed, listening intently to Ann's readings, trying to analyze each comment his wife had supposedly made to Rosalie, trying to find every little nuance that would convince him it was actually his Sarah speaking.

"And that's it, Lucas. Everything that came through."

Lucas sat for a long time, not moving, barely breathing. Finally, he raised his head and turned to Ann. He reached and took her hand.

"There were a few things that were uttered that could well have been Sarah speaking. If that is true, then I've got to see Rosalie again. I'll admit I'm starting to believe in what you've been telling me. And that is very difficult for me to say. When Sarah said that I lost her twice, Rosalie couldn't have known that I had lost her to dementia first, and Rosalie didn't ever question what was being said. They were statements. No questions. Ann, do you think it was Sarah?"

"I *know* it was Sarah, Lucas. And do you remember what Rosalie said to you as we were leaving?"

Lucas thought, then shook his head.

"Rosalie told you she would be seeing you again."

Lucas stood up from the table and, still holding Ann's hand, gently got her to stand also. Then he moved close, took her in his arms, and held her. In seconds Ann responded, giving a hug back.

"Thank you," he whispered in her ear.

Ann responded softly, "You are so welcome."

• • • • •

"Bedtime!" Ann called out from the living room. While Lucas was cleaning up the kitchen and washing the few dirty dishes and implements, she had made up the sofa bed with sheets, blankets, and a pillow. Lucas saw what she had done and thought it looked very comfortable. He would soon be dead to the world anyway, after their exhausting day.

"Ann, that looks great! Thank you so much. You have made this an unforgettable day. I'll have to sleep in my shorts. They're clean! Unless you have a nightie that might fit." He and Ann laughed and he felt good. His sensed a lessening of his grief.

"That's all right, sir. I'll leave the heat on a little. You should be good." She blew him a kiss, waved goodnight, and gave him a look of longing which he didn't recognize. Then she retreated into her bedroom.

Lucas took off his clothes, glancing furtively every so often at her closed bedroom door, afraid it might open for some reason.

As he slipped between the sheets, another thought came to mind. Sarah had always told him he snored! He didn't want to snore here. He had heard it said that by sleeping on your side you wouldn't snore. He would do just that. Turn his back to the room and face the wall. That should work. His session with Rosalie came back into his thoughts and more private concerns regarding the whole process came to mind, thoughts that he alone would have to deal with and find answers for. Ann could only do so much and she had done so much already.

As thoughts of the day kept sleep away, James began to formulate plans to find the answers he needed. Some of the answers, anyway. Eventually sleep, like another blanket, covered him.

Ann couldn't sleep either; she didn't know why. She tossed and turned, making a bundle out of her blankets. What was wrong with her? Thoughts of Lucas McNab, *her boss* for God's sake, sleeping here, in her living room, practically right next to her. She shook her head. 'Lord, I'm acting like a teenager with a crush on the school hockey star.' She eventually had to get up and remake her bed. She crawled back in. 'Now, get some sleep, you idiot!'

The aroma of coffee slowly brought Lucas awake. Ann, still in her robe, was busy putting together breakfast for two, an entirely new experience for her, and she was thoroughly enjoying the challenge.

She heard Lucas stirring in the living room. "Wakey, wakey, sleepyhead!" she called. "Everything you need is in the bathroom."

"Thanks," Lucas managed to croak. He grabbed his pants from the hassock and quickly put them on, keeping a wary eye on the kitchen area. He made his way through Ann's bedroom, noticing the rumpled sheets and blankets as he passed her bed, and he felt a longing for Sarah. He went through his ablutions, scrubbed his teeth with cold water, and padded out to the kitchen.

"How did you sleep?" Ann asked.

"Pretty well, after I managed to get to sleep. Had a lot on my mind."

With her back to him, Ann had a smile on her face when she heard that.

"One question... did I snore?"

"If you did, I didn't hear you. Coffee? Are you a breakfast person? I was going to make some toast, do an egg. What would you like?"

"Coffee and toast suits me fine."

Ann poured a large coffee and took a plate of toast out of the oven where she had been keeping it warm. She placed it on the table, poured herself a coffee, and sat down at the other end of the table.

"What's the day look like? More snow? Did we get much more last night?" Lucas asked.

"Actually, a warm front developed and took a lot of the snow. Looks like the roads will be in good shape." Ann took a piece of toast to nibble on.

There was silence between them for several minutes. Then Lucas looked intently at Ann. "Ann, I have a plan I would like to try today."

Ann said nothing and just stared at him, waiting to hear his plan.

"Here's what I'd like to do. I'm feeling some guilt about not going back to the firm. So, to clear that up, a little, I would like you to go to work this morning. I will call Matt and explain to him that I want to start to work, but to ease back in, I want you to pick up some files and bring them to the house. I'll identify some files for Matt and you can get them from him. I'll tell Matt I need you to help me. Now, that's not really lying, not yet, anyway. Follow me so far? Your work isn't over yet. I want you to call Rosalie, at an appropriate time, but early as possible, and make an appointment for me to see her. Not for a reading, mind. I just want to talk. There are some aspects of this I've got to clear up in my mind. Are you good with that, Ann? I just want a visit with Rosalie."

Excitement showed on Ann's face. "You bet," Ann replied. "What time is it?"

Lucas finished a second coffee and some toast while Ann dressed. She was fast, and they were on the road by 8:30. She waited at Lucas' house while he called Matt Clark at his office. Lucas knew he would be there. He was always the first to arrive at work. He made arrangements for Ann to pick up specific files. Matt was pleased that Lucas was starting work again and agreed with him that this was a good way to ease back into the 'harness'.

Ann left for the office, arriving shortly after 9:15. After some small talk with Matt, she took the files and returned to the parking lot. Before she got back into the Jeep, she made the call to Rosalie and set up a time to meet with her. Driving back to the house, she enjoying this feeling like she was part of an *X-Files* episode. She parked her Jeep on the right side of the driveway, beside the Equinox, knowing

Lucas would be driving today. Fortunately, the mild weather had slid most of the snow off his vehicle.

While Ann was doing her thing, Lucas had a quick shower and dressed in casual clothes, trying to organize his thoughts all the while. He was pulling on a lightweight knit vest over his dress shirt as Ann came in with the files.

"Did you manage to call Rosalie?"

"I did. Your meeting is set for 11:00 this morning. We should take something for dinner, Lucas."

"Good idea. What do you suggest?"

"What about picking up some seafood chowder? She is not likely a big eater, especially not at noon."

"Good choice. We'll do that."

The drive to Prospect was relatively short compared to yesterday. They arrived at Rosalie's little blue house only ten minutes early. Lucas let Ann out at the front door as he had to ride the SUV up a snowbank to clear the road. He jumped clear of the snow, almost, and joined Ann at the door. They were about to knock when Rosalie opened the door with a big friendly smile on her face.

"Come in, come in." Rosalie back-pedalled to allow her two guests to enter the small hallway. They inhaled the wonderful aroma of freshly baked bread. The house was warm, almost too warm for Lucas. He already regretted wearing the sleeveless vest. Ann quickly took off her short length car coat, along with her scarf. She was starting to feel a bit uncomfortable too. Rosalie recognized the situation and apologized while opening the back door, letting in some cool, fresh air. "These old wood stoves are great for cooking on, but the heat from them is pretty hard to control." She returned to the hallway, saying, "It's so good to see you both again. How are the roads this morning?"

"The drive was very good. The temperature change got rid of a lot of snow overnight," replied Ann.

"Well," Rosalie said, "if this isn't a reading, what's it all about, pray tell?"

At this point Lucas eased around Ann and explained their reason for being there again so soon.

"Rosalie, after the reading yesterday, I had so many questions that I just had to talk with you again. I hope that is all right and that we're not imposing on you."

"Well, I'm not just sure what I can tell you, but let's sit down and I'll see what I can do to help you. I just made a pot of tea. Can I pour you a cup?"

Not really wanting something hot, they nonetheless acquiesced and each said yes.

After everybody was settled in around Rosalie's little table, Lucas began.

"Rosalie, I would like, very much, to learn more about your ability as a medium, and everything you can tell me about, well... everything! I am just amazed at your ability."

"Well, Mr. McNab, Lucas, like I told you yesterday, when my husband, Edgar, was lost at sea twenty-six years ago, I was completely devastated. I almost died. Fortunately, we're a very close community here and I had great support. Of course, there were others who were lost too. Two other men, along with my Edgar. Well, it was a short time after I recovered from my loss that I started seeing and getting messages from people who had passed! Let me tell you, it scared the..." Rosalie searched for a polite expletive to emphasize the importance of this development, "...devil out of me. I didn't know what was happening!" Rosalie took a sip of her tea. "But to be perfectly honest, I think I had a little bit of this ability all my life."

Lucas was listening intently to Rosalie's story. "Rosalie, when did you begin your 'mediumship', if there is such a word? Like, when did you begin to 'read' people?"

"Well, it happened quite by accident, really. You see, I never saw the people who talked to me, not like I see you here. It was like they were in a fog or something. Then, one day at the post office, this lady came in. I didn't know her at all, but all of a sudden, a man came forward in my mind's eye, and indicated he wanted to talk to this lady. He claimed to be her father. He told me to ask her about Kelly. So, I did just that, after introducing myself and explaining what was happening, you know. Well, when I mentioned the name 'Kelly', well, she was shocked. You wouldn't believe it. Well, it turned out to be her son who had passed recently in a car accident. We had a little reading right there. And, of course, as people came in, they'd stop and listen to what I had to say. And when I was finished, there was quite a bunch of people around me. So, the fox was in the chicken coop then, and I've been doing readings ever since. I believe I've helped some people with their grief. Hope so, anyway."

"That's amazing, Rosalie. How do you receive the messages from... the other side, so to speak?"

"Well, Lucas, I don't know if I can explain it. They just seem to speak right at me. I don't have trouble understanding them at all. That's about all I can say about that."

"And do you see the people clearly now? You mentioned earlier that they appeared to be in a fog. Are they still that way, or do you seem them like you see us?"

"Oh, they're all very clear now. They're not exactly like I can see you, but they look pretty good. I can easily tell who it is if I've known them before, like."

"Rosalie, how do you feel when you get these messages? Do you feel different at all?"

"Well, Lucas, when I am getting a message, it's something like when you get a feeling of having to do something. Like a strong feeling of what's right and wrong. You understand? Like a wave flowing over you. I think it's their energy meeting my energy, like the energies are talking to each other. That's about all I know about that."

Ann interrupted the discussion and suggested it was time for a bite to eat. Lucas exhaled, as if he'd been holding his breath the whole time.

"Oh, my dear, I've got fresh baked bread."

"And we brought some chowder that would go deliciously with your bread. What do you say?" Ann asked.

"Well, that sounds grand, dear."

Lucas went to the SUV and got the chowder. Taking it to the kitchen, he said to Rosalie, "We'll have to heat this up a little."

"No problem, child." She searched under the cupboard. Bringing out a large pot, she proceeded to pour the containers of chowder in, very carefully. "This will heat up in no time at all."

As the chowder simmered, its seafood aroma mingled with the sweet smell of the fresh bread, both wrapped in the comforting warmth and crackling sounds coming from the old wood stove. This combination carried Ann away! Even Lucas came back to the kitchen to get closer to the ambrosia.

All three of them settled in around Rosalie's little table, now holding bowls of chowder, a large basket of fresh bread, and the ever-present cups of tea. Ann and Lucas commented that it was the finest meal they had enjoyed in a long time. Rosalie didn't show much emotion but there was just a slight gleam of satisfaction in her eyes. She enjoyed this couple, Ann and Lucas. They seemed genuine and good folks. And she was taken with the sincere interest Lucas had with her ability to read the spirits. She was old news in the village and it was exciting that she had sparked Lucas' interest. She had to admit that it spiced up her quiet, village life. Edgar would be happy for her.

As much as he was enjoying the lunch, it didn't deter Lucas from his reason for being here. Between spoonfuls of chowder, he was unrelenting with his queries to Rosalie, but in a nice, quiet, respectful way.

"Rosalie, I'm sure you have encountered folks who just don't believe in all of this that you do. How do you react to those people?"

"Well, Lucas, I'm no minister and I'm not trying to convert anybody to this. I can't change their minds, nor would I want to. You know how it all works. I'm just a means of getting messages to those people who are looking for them. If I can help a person by putting them in contact with a loved one, and that helps them in some way, then I'm happy to do that. Let me ask you something, Lucas. How did you react after your reading yesterday? Do you believe in the messages I gave you, or are you not sure? Why did you come here again today?"

Lucas was somewhat taken aback by Rosalie's questions. They were certainly legitimate ones.

"To be truthful, Rosalie, I'm about half and half on everything. And I'm hoping you can give me answers. Answers that will take me to that other half and complete the picture for me."

"I'll do my best for you, Lucas." Rosalie looked at him and she saw the sincerity in his face.

Lucas knew Rosalie had more to say, and that she knew more than she was letting on. Would he be able to tap into that knowledge? Rosalie had years of experience doing this and he had to know more. This was becoming his Holy Grail.

"Here's a question for you, Rosalie. Why do you think you happen to have this very unique ability to receive messages from... dead people? Sorry, I don't mean to be crude."

"Well, Lucas, I truly have no idea. It's like it just picked me. Mind you, my ability has developed and improved over the years. It seems the more I do it, the better it gets. Just like most things, I guess. But I will tell you that it is real. I've experienced way too much to ever say otherwise. All I can really tell you is that after the sad loss of my husband, and as I slowly learned how to get along without Edgar, this whole thing started about seeing people in my mind, like they come out of the shadows, you see. And they started talking to me or something. I could hardly understand them in the beginning. And it was just like I told you about what happened at the post office that day. Would anybody like more tea?"

After Rosalie refilled their cups, Lucas continued his questions. "Now, Rosalie. Have you ever experienced where the spirits or souls go when they leave the body? Have you ever seen this place?"

Rosalie didn't answer him immediately. She reacted to the question by looking out the little front window with the faded yellow curtains. She remained that way for a short while before speaking.

"Yes, Lucas, I have seen the other side. And I can tell you, what little I saw was simply beautiful. It was something I had never seen. There was a beautiful light everywhere. Everything was so very bright and beautiful. I wanted to go there, Lucas. Flowers were so big and so pretty. I saw my Edgar and he was fishing. He gave me a big wave and smiled. He looked much younger too. I sure hope you get to see it, Lucas. You too, Ann. I mean just in a reading, like!"

Ann was behind the scenes the whole time. This day belonged to Lucas, but she paid close attention to everything, and Rosalie's answer to Lucas' last question left her awestruck.

Everyone was silent now. Lucas and Ann were trying to imagine for themselves the picture Rosalie placed in their minds. They were both mute for several minutes, and then something completely unexpected happened.

"Lucas, your wife is here. She says she will try to leave signs to let you know she is around you. She tells me, 'Tell him how thankful I am for all our years together.' She says this is like being on holiday. She says she will bring you some sign. She mentions living on an extended world cruise ship. She says go and do whatever makes you happy. 'But remember,' she says, 'you're only on loan to somebody else' - you still belong to her. She is very happy. She tells you 'Don't get attached to things. All that truly matters is found in the heart.'

"She's leaving and she blows you a kiss."

Lucas was having difficulty breathing and tears blurred his vision. He was in shock. He left the table and went outside to be alone. He couldn't take in what had just happened. It was so unexpected. And it sounded so like his Sarah.

Ann opened the door behind him. "Are you okay, Lucas?" She had been wiping her eyes too and a slight redness was evident.

Lucas turned to Ann and she could see mixed emotions in his face. He moved the few steps toward her and simply hung his arms over her shoulders and stayed close. She placed her arms lightly around his waist and waited. Lucas had given in. He didn't need any more questions and answers. Rosalie was for real and so were her messages. All doubt was gone now with that one brief contact with his wife.

• • • • •

The drive back to the city was relatively slow and very quiet. Ann glanced over at Lucas every once in a while to see if he was all right. Seeing him staring straight ahead at the road, Ann hoped he was seeing the road and not letting his thoughts take him somewhere else. Eventually, she had to break into the silence and she did it very softly.

"Lucas, are you okay? Want to talk? Want to stop somewhere for coffee?" She kept her eyes on him looking for some indication he was still with her.

Lucas tilted his head slightly towards Ann and just as softly, said, "What was that, Ann? Did you say something?"

"I was just checking to see if you were okay. You seemed deep in thought. Do you want to stop somewhere?"

"I guess I was. We'll have something when we get back. All right?" Lucas ran his fingers through his hair to help bring him back to the present.

"Sure. We're almost there now."

Lucas felt quite drained of energy as he turned into his driveway and parked beside Ann's Jeep. His legs barely held him up as he stepped out of the SUV. He put his arm around Ann's shoulders as they walked to the front door. He unlocked the door and opened it for Ann to enter the foyer. She stopped, unzipped her knee-high boots, and slipped them off. He walked by her into the kitchen, thinking it was too early for scotch. Then he rethought that decision: 'Is it ever too early in the day for scotch? he wondered. He went through the ritual of making brewed coffee. Ann came into the kitchen that she knew very well from all the visits she had made over the years. She went to the cupboard and took out two large mugs, then to the fridge for milk. She looked at Lucas. He was leaning on the edge of the sink, staring out the kitchen window into the back yard. Having a pretty good idea of what he was experiencing, she felt a closeness to him at this moment. She wanted to be near him, to comfort him, to help ease his mind.

The coffee maker stopped perking and the resulting silence shook them both out of their reverie.

Lucas took the coffee pot to the table and filled both mugs. Ann put in just enough milk to colour it the way he liked it. She had come to like it the same way. They both sat down at the kitchen table.

Suddenly, Ann exclaimed, "Lucas! I didn't take notes!"

"It's okay, Ann. I remember it all. Very clearly."

They sipped the hot coffee in silence. They were both reliving the hours with Rosalie.

Finally, Lucas turned, looked into Ann's eyes and spoke. "Ann, I now know what it was you were trying to get me to understand. The importance of it and the necessity of it. You can call me a believer now. And it wasn't anything really, that Rosalie said, although I believe she is a genuine medium, if not a psychic medium. No. It was when Sarah came through that made me a firm believer. Something she said that nobody could know. I'll explain.

"A short while before Sarah passed, we had read somewhere about this old lady talking about all the advantages of retiring on a round-the-world cruise ship compared to living in a retirement home. Free meals, all you can eat; sheets changed every day; free medical; and so on and so on, and she compared it to the costs of living in a retirement home and how much cheaper it would be. She described the beautiful stops at tropical ports. We thought it was a great idea, and we would bring it up every so often and have a laugh over it. Actually, it made a lot of sense. She ended her story by saying that if you died on board, which would happen, they simply threw you overboard!

"Well, Sarah brought up that very cruise ship. Remember? That was her validation to me that she, her soul, lives!" Lucas was wide-eyed and took hold of Ann's arm. "Jeez, I was in shock, let me tell you. That is a monumental revelation, for me!" he was twisting and turning in his chair. He wanted to jump up and down and shout Hallelujah!

" I am now a confirmed believer, and I owe it all to you. How can I ever repay you for this?"

"You don't have to thank me, Lucas. I know how empowering the realization can be and I'm so happy you have made the connection!" She reached over and took his hand and saw a tear form in Lucas' eyes. She ached to hold him close.

Lucas stood up from the table, coffee mug in hand. "Let's go to the sunroom. I hope you'll be a good listener, 'cause I've got a lot on my mind tonight."

$$\bullet \quad \bullet \quad \bullet \quad \bullet \quad \bullet$$

They sat in the soft leather chairs, sipping their coffees and staring at the flames of the little electric fireplace, both deep in their own thoughts. They stayed like this for several long minutes until Lucas placed his mug on the table between them. Turning to face Ann, he began.

"Ann, I can't remember ever being this excited and confused at the same time. I've got so many thoughts and questions running around in my head; I don't know where I am. I've had to do a three-sixty in my thinking. A complete turn around. If this was a court case I would have to excuse myself. And I've got you to thank for it all!" Lucas made a feeble gesture of being mad at Ann, smiling, and she smiled back.

Ann watched Lucas intently as he spoke. She was so pleased that he had made the turn, so to speak, that she realized she now understood what the expression, "turning inside out" meant. That was the measure of wonderful happiness she was experiencing. She was that happy.

Lucas continued. "But I have got to learn more, about everything concerning this transition that takes place. Rosalie, bless her heart, did so much in this regard, but she isn't able to take me to where I need to go. She's the introduction. Now I have got to find someone who can take me deeper into understanding what is going on. Can you see that, Ann?"

"I understand exactly what you're saying, Lucas. You are going to have to find, for use of a better word, a modern medium. One who has studied and educated themselves in this paranormal field. It's not going to be easy. Remember what I told you - how choosing a medium is like buying a used car. It will take some research, but, hey, it'll be no different than working on a court case. Lord knows we've got experience in researching!"

"You know, you're absolutely right. It's no different." The mention of a court case had brought Lucas' mind into sharp focus regarding his responsibility to the law firm that paid his salary. "Speaking of court cases, I've got to get back to the office. I'm sure I can handle myself before a judge now." Lucas studied the fireplace intently. What he had just discovered about spirits and the afterlife sure as hell beat whatever awaited him at Brannigan and Clark. He knew he wouldn't be able to let go of what he had discovered, and yet there was his obligation to the firm. He did owe them, after all. How could he balance the two? He had some money in the bank. Sarah's insurances were part of that. He could get by for a while. He had no outstanding debts, which was good.

"Nickel for your thoughts," asked Ann curiously.

"I've been trying to get a handle on a few things, like getting back to the office, which I don't really want to do just yet. I'm quite capable of returning to the practice, mind you. But my interest is not there. My interest is with the spirit world. Now, how do you think that statement would go over with Wiff Brannigan, I ask you?"

Actually, Ann had been thinking about the same problem.

"Lucas, what about this. You must have some vacation coming to you. This time that you've been away falls under 'compassionate leave'. Plus, what about taking an extended leave from the firm, unpaid of course. They couldn't really refuse a request like that, could they?"

Lucas furrowed his brow as he tried to find faults in Ann's suggestions.

"By damn, girl, that all makes sense. I can manage unpaid leave okay. But I want you with me on this. The whole way. What can we do about that part?"

She thought for a minute. "I've got a little vacation time coming to me. Not much, but some."

They both sat and stared into the paper flames.

"Listen. I'll go to the office tomorrow and start things moving. Leave it with me. I'll manage something. We've got to make this happen," Lucas decided. "Would you like a glass of wine?"

• • • • •

When Lucas arrived at the law firm, it was as if he hadn't ever left. Just a normal day at the office. Ann was already there so he gave her the files from yesterday to store away. They exchanged a few pleasantries and were soon back in their roles of 'boss' and 'assistant'.

Matthew Clark was already in his office, being the first to come in to work. Lucas thought he should take the opportunity to approach Matt alone, thinking it would be easier than having to deal with Wiff too. Why was he feeling guilty, like a little boy attempting to skip school? Everything he planned to do was above board. 'It must be the thought that I can't give my reasons for my actions,' Lucas reasoned. 'Keeping secrets from good friends. But it can't be any other way.'

Lucas approached Matt and asked, "Matt, can I have a word with you?"

"Good morning, Lucas. Ready for work, are you? Come in. Let's talk."

Lucas got the distinct feeling that Matt knew something was afoot.

"I would like to take my vacation days now, and I'm asking if I can have an extended leave, without pay, of course, for a couple of weeks. There are things I've got to attend to." Now that wasn't a lie.

"That all shouldn't be a problem, Lucas. I'll have Barb in finance set it up today. Will you be going out of town at all? Not that we should need to contact you, or anything like that. And it's none of my business anyway."

"I'll be away for a time, Matt. There's one more thing I have to ask about. Ann…"

"There's the man, himself! How ya doin' Lucas? Yer lookin' good." Damn. Wiff showed up.

"Good morning, Wiff. I'm feeling a lot better today."

"Lucas here is taking his vacation time," Matt explained. "I think it's a good idea, myself. Don't you, Wiff?"

"Why sure. A perfect time. Ya gotta clear yer head after somethin' like this happens," Wiff nodded in understanding.

"He's also asked for a leave of absence, without pay, for a few weeks, to attend to personal matters. Right, Lucas?" Matt asked.

Lucas nodded affirmation in Wiff's direction.

"Well, I don't see nothin' against that there," Wiff said agreeably.

Lucas had to face the difficult part now. "This might be way out of line, but I'd like for Ann to… well, help me out with some things… be with me, like." Man, they're not going to go for this at all.

"Aha," Wiff grunted, with a slight leer on his face. He looked sideways at Lewis with a knowing, *wink, wink.* "Now, how's this gonna all work out here?"

"She must have some vacation time coming too," Lucas ventured.

"Ann, Ann… could ya come in here fer just a minute?" Wiff was setting Lucas up for some kidding, Lucas knew.

Ann quickly entered the office. She looked briefly at Lucas but tried to maintain an air of innocence. "Yes, Mr. Brannigan?"

Lucas could see what was coming from Wiff Brannigan, and it wasn't going to be pretty. Wiff had that condescending air about himself that only Wiff could carry off.

"Ann, Lucas here is askin' fer some time off. Nothin' wrong with that. Did ya know he was doin' this? 'Cause he's askin' fer you too."

"Lucas asked me to help him settle personal business, yes."Ann could feel the colour rising in her face. 'Dear God, let this end soon!' she prayed.

"I think that's about all we need to know, Wiff. I'll get Barb to settle this all up. Ann, you can see Barb about the details. And Lucas, don't be too long, will you?" Matt settled the matter.

"Now Lucas, you jus' get done what ya gotta do and we'll see ya back here soon," Wiff said. Then he patted Lucas' shoulder and gave him a big, exaggerated wink. "An don't do anythin' that me or Lewis would'n do." He gave a throaty chuckle as he left the office.

"I'm sorry about all that, Lucas, and I sincerely apologize to you, Ann, for Wiff's insensitivity."

"That's okay; it's just Wiff being Wiff, is all. Thanks for doing this for me, Matt. I'll make it up to you," Lucas shook Matt's hand.

"Good luck, Lucas."

• • • • •

After picking up their cheques and tidying up their offices, Ann and Lucas made their way to Tim Hortons in Scotia Square Mall via the Link. The weather had turned blustery and cold, making the enclosed 'pedway' a real blessing.

They took their coffees to a table. Lucas looked seriously at Ann and his face slowly formed a large grin. With excitement showing in her eyes, Ann returned the grin. They were like two teenagers skipping class, like two sweethearts in love. Both felt as if a gate had opened before them, and the world was theirs. Lucas couldn't believe how accommodating Matt, and even Wiff, had been.

Lucas broke the euphoric setting. "Okay. Now, how are we going to go about this?"

"Well, what is it you want to find out, Lucas?"

"Here's where I'm at. I'm pretty well convinced of an afterlife. I now believe in the souls of those who cross over, that they exist… somewhere, though I don't yet know where. Firstly, I think I'd like to have another independent reading, from a more modern medium, like we talked about. That will be our start. Secondly, if possible, I want proof of some sort, of an afterlife. How's that sound? Doable, do you think?"

"Ummm, sounds like a real challenge. The second part more so."

They finished their coffees and made their way to the parking lot. Lucas had suggested they go to his house and start drawing up a 'battle plan', as he termed it. Soup and sandwiches made up their lunch, after which they settled down in the usual friendly sunroom.

"Ann, now don't take this the wrong way, but wouldn't it be easier if you stayed here instead of driving back and forth? It would save a lot of time and there's a spare bed, as you know. What do you think?" And then he could see Wiff Brannigan's knowing leer. 'Damn him. It's not like that, is it?' he asked himself.

Ann tried to look reserved and found it difficult. "That does make sense, doesn't it? I'll have to go home and pick up some things though." She was nervous and excited at the same time. 'Good Lord,' she thought. 'What just happened?'

"Okay, then. You get what you want, and I'll make up the spare bedroom. If you would, Ann, stop and pick up what you think we could use in the food line." He passed her a hundred-dollar bill. He was pretty sure he had enough wine and scotch.

Lucas tidied up the spare room. He vacuumed the carpet and dusted where he thought he should, made sure the drawers in the small dresser were empty and clean, reset the clock from reading 12;00, 12;00, 12;00, and finally found an extra blanket and placed it on the foot of the bed. 'There,' he thought. 'That should do it.'

As he waited for Ann to return, Lucas recalled the messages Rosalie had received from Sarah. He thought of the one that told him she was bringing another woman into his life so he wouldn't be lonely. Smiling, he recalled his Sarah saying, 'Just remember, you're only on loan. You still belong to me!' And he wondered, 'Was Ann going to be the woman Sarah had mentioned? Could be,' he mused. She had been fulfilling the role for the last few days already.

Ann arrived back at the house in the late afternoon. She had to make two trips to get everything in from the Jeep, including her suitcase. Lucas was busy peeling the shells off of the shrimp he had quickly thawed, so he wasn't any help to Ann.

"Hey there. Watcha doin'?"

"Working on supper, and these damn shrimp are really cold. How'd you make out?"

"Managed to get everything. It's really turning frigid. Might have more snow by morning."

"I got the spare room fixed up a little. You can put your things in there. The drawers in the vanity are all empty."

After storing the groceries in their proper places, Ann picked up her suitcase and made her way to the spare room while Lucas emptied a bottle of Alfredo and garlic pasta sauce into a pot. He grabbed another pot, partially filled it with water, measured roughly an amount of Somen noodles he thought would be enough for both of them, and set them aside until the water boiled. The shrimp would be ready then also.

"Umm. That smells delicious, Lucas. How's about I make us a couple of drinks?"

"Great idea. You know where everything is, eh?"

Ann went to the little liquor cabinet and took the scotch and a partial bottle of white wine to the table, poured a wine for herself and made a scotch for Lucas. After the shrimp were added to the sauce, Lucas reached over for a nip of the scotch.

When everything was ready, Lucas made up two plates and set them on placemats on the table.

"Should have made a salad to go with this," he commented.

"This is wonderful. Sit down and relax," Ann suggested.

After their meal and a quick clean-up of the kitchen, they refilled their glasses and moved to the 'war room' as Lucas had dubbed the sunroom.

"Okay, expert. Tell me how we go about locating a bona fide psychic medium, oh wise one," Lucas began lightheartedly.

"We could start by looking in the Yellow Pages. They do advertise, you know. And the only sure way of determining legitimacy is to have a reading done. I think some will do a so-called sample of their ability, if they're any good. We could start with the Yellow Pages. Or there's the internet too."

"That's right. Never considered the 'net. How dense of me! Let's try it, Ann."

Ann moved to the chair in front of the monitor in Lucas' 'computer room' opened up the keyboard and turned on Lucas' old desktop computer. She typed in '*mediums Nova Scotia*,' and up came the sites. They both read the descriptions of each site, Lucas leaning as close to Ann as he dared.

"Let's try this one," Ann said as she moved the cursor to her choice.

"Jeez, look! There must be fifteen, twenty listed there. And that's just one site," exclaimed Lucas.

"Bet the majority of them are from the States. You have to really be careful, Lucas. So many scams out there. If you're not completely aware of what's going on, you can really be taken for a ride. Some will say, 'Oh, you should have another reading,' or they'll lead you on, get you crying and at your weakest, and all sorts of crap! I know there are psychic fairs held around the province, but I believe we're too early for those. That would have been the ideal way to locate a good medium. We'll keep searching here. See what we come up with."

"Well, Ann, we haven't time to check out too many. I just want an honest reading to, you know, sort of compare with Rosalie, and talk about the afterlife. I'll top up your glass while you look."

Lucas brought in their drinks, pulled up a chair next to Ann, and started reading the screen.

Their glasses were just about empty when Ann exclaimed, "This one sounds really good, Lucas," and she proceeded to read off the information she had found.

"'East coast psychic medium, Marie St-Onge. I was born with a gift that allows me to communicate with souls who have passed on.'

"And listen to this, Lucas: *'I am a firm believer in life after ₁eath'*! This sounds like a really good start to our search. She goes on about hosting live events across the province - all the same info. We want a private session with her, right?"

"Exactly, Ann. Where is she located?"

"She gives a Dartmouth address. Sixteen Lakefront Road, apartment 201."

"I believe those apartments are right on Maynard Lake. I know where that is. Does she give a number to call? See if you can set up an appointment for a reading,"

Ann made the call and after a brief discussion obtained an appointment for the next afternoon, at 1:30. They toasted their success and couldn't hide the excitement for the upcoming reading. Lucas felt this might be a turning point in his quest for proof of an afterlife. At least, it should be a push in the right direction.

With the reading tomorrow confirmed, the next thing was to determine exactly what it was Lucas wanted to learn. Having no background on the afterlife, he would be at the mercy at Marie St-Onge. And that was okay. He would have her perspective as a start, at the very least. He would simply play it by ear, with Ann dutifully taking notes. They both headed to bed relatively early. Emotionally, they were tired. It had been a busy day and a lot was accomplished.

Ann made her way to the spare bedroom Lucas had prepared. She looked forward to a good night's rest in anticipation of tomorrow. She hadn't had time to realize the closeness just established between she and Lucas. She wondered if he had. She pulled on her nightie and slipped under the covers, 'perchance to dream?'

Lucas put off going to bed. He wanted to be alone, but with Sarah, he hoped. A new relationship was developing between he and his wife that he didn't fully understand. Here he was, grounded on this mundane, crazy world, and there was Sarah, apparently alive, or he should say her soul or spirit was alive, on a completely different level, somewhere. How do you reconcile all that in your mind? He had so many questions and was looking for answers.

"Sarah, I need to hear from you tomorrow. Please dear, be there with me. I really can use your help." Just then he heard the strident wail of an ambulance and he shuddered. Some unfortunate family is having a terrible life-altering experience, and he knew exactly what they were going through. He listened, hoping to hear the siren keep going. That would mean nobody on his street was involved. He fought back the memories of Sarah's many trips to the hospital as he walked slowly up the stairs to his empty bed.

• • • • •

Lucas was up early and Ann could smell the breakfast being put together as she made her way down to the kitchen.

"Ummmmm, that smells sooo good. Whatcha making, Lucas?"

"Oh, just throwing some things together." Lucas had developed cooking skills out of necessity and had become quite good. In fact, he had discovered he rather enjoyed cooking. It had become something else to occupy his mind. Another distraction.

"Sit right down here, miss, and try my ruby-red grapefruit, smothered in Drambuie with a light dusting of brown sugar, and warmed just until the sugar melts. That will be followed with French toast imbued with a banana sauce, slathered in maple syrup. All of this tempting faire is topped off with fresh pressed coffee. Tips are graciously accepted!" He whispered in Ann's ear, "The flowers are plastic, I'm afraid."

Ann gave Lucas a broad smile and marvelled at his presentation. And everything tasted as good as it looked, or even better.

"Lucas, my dear, you're going to spoil me! How will I ever be able to go back to my little apartment, after all this?"

"Just enjoy it while you can. You never know how long things last nowadays."

They spent the rest of the morning cleaning up the kitchen and preparing nervously for the afternoon meeting with Marie St-Onge. It was agreed that Lucas would have his reading first and, if Ms. St-Onge agreed, spend a second hour questioning her on the afterlife and other points that might come to mind.

• • • • •

Lucas crossed to Dartmouth via the MacDonald bridge, took the Wyse Road exit to Windmill Road until it came to the Portland Street branch, and followed it up to Lakefront Road on the left.

The long row of three-storey brick apartments still looked to be in very good shape, being more than sixty years old. Lucas slowly drove up the slight grade of Lakefront, with both Lucas and Ann screening the buildings' numbers until they saw number 46. There was a small parking area at the foot of the short flight of steps leading to the front entrance. Lucas pulled into a parking spot, hoping it wasn't assigned to anyone in particular.

They entered the building, located the stairwell, and proceeded to the second level. Lucas knocked lightly on the door of apartment 201. Almost immediately the door opened wide and Marie St-Onge smiled and invited them in.

She was a striking woman, about the age of Ann, Lucas ventured. She had raven black hair with a natural white streak on one side by her face. She was dressed in a floor length black dress with a white Asian design. Adorned with a large white beaded necklace and a matching bracelet on her left wrist, she wore no makeup that Lucas could tell, and she didn't need it, he thought.

Ann was taking this all in also, but she was more interested in how Lucas was responding to this 'vision'. Was she actually jealous of Marie St-Onge? It was an unfamiliar feeling so she wasn't sure.

"Come in, won't you? Please, make yourselves comfortable. Can I get you anything to drink?"

Lucas and Ann sat together on the grey sofa and both declined her offer. Marie came in and sat opposite them in the matching grey armchair.

"Now, who is having the reading?" she asked.

"I am," Lucas said, at the same time as Ann indicated it would be him.

"So, Lucas, may I call you Lucas? Have you been to a medium before, or is this your first time?"

"I have had a reading before," Lucas said.

"Then you have an idea of how this will be conducted. I detected a sense of some urgency on the phone. Might I ask what has prompted you to contact me?"

Lucas felt an air of suspicion around Marie, and he thought it best to be honest right up front. "When we read your ad, Ms. St-Onge, there was something you said that is very important to me. You stated you were a firm believer in the afterlife. I am a recent convert to the same belief and I am searching for proof of that very thing."

Marie St-Onge relaxed a little when she heard Lucas' explanation. "Lucas, they are, they have been, searching for that proof... forever. It seems not to matter to those who disbelieve in all that we do - proving that there *is* a place where the souls or spirits exist. The 'debunkers', as they have been called, have to see and touch this space that the spirits occupy. So, you are up against cynics and people with completely closed minds, and I sincerely wish you the best of luck. Now, shall we move to the table in the kitchen for your reading? It might be a little cramped but it will be adequate."

As they arranged themselves around the round, glass-topped table, Ann drew her chair away to leave Marie and Lucas facing each other. Ann was relieved to see that Marie used a CD recorder, and assumed the CD would be theirs. This would relieve her of having to take notes.

"Is there a particular person you would like to speak to?" Marie asked Lucas.

"Not at present. First, I'd like to see who comes through."

Marie lowered her head and closed her eyes.

"I hear your name being called. I have a woman coming through. This is a younger woman. I have a name that begins with 'S'. Sally, Shirley. She claims to be your wife."

"Sarah," Lucas said, and wondered why Sarah would be younger.

"She says your grief is trapped inside. Go to a secluded place and talk out loud or yell. Show your grief. Let it out. She is full of joy. She enjoys her memories of teaching."

Marie looked at Ann and Lucas. "You know, grief is a selfish action and, in some cases, can even hold a soul back from making the transition. In fact, the person grieving is feeling sorry for themselves. Traditional funerals... well, I won't go there.

"Sarah's transition was very emotional. It wasn't easy for her to let go. She says for you to be more joyful. Don't dwell on sadness. She tells you not to conform to other people. Be yourself. She acknowledges you having conversations with her.

"Now, that is very important, talking with those who have crossed over. Prayers too are a help. Meditation. All important to our loved ones who have crossed over.

"She says she took the age of thirty-five when she crossed over. She is in her prime. She loves to read and only has to think about reading to be able to.

"When you are in a deep sleep, she comes and takes your spirit on trips to concerts and historic places. She takes you all over the world. The lectures include all aspects of a topic, such as watching the pyramids being built. She takes you right down to the villages and towns. All the senses are included. It is very similar to... do you remember the Christmas movie about Scrooge that starred Alastair

Sim? And one of the ghosts took him on a flying journey to the future? It's like that, only more pleasant!" And Marie smiled.

"She is always around you. She follows you around the kitchen. She gives you a lobster. Claw meat is the only good part, she says."

Lucas' emotions were coiled like a spring. 'Sarah is here! She is talking to me again!' he thought to himself.

"Sarah has a brightness to her. She sees the song *You are the Sunshine of my Life* around you. She says you were a source of comfort for her when she was ill.

"Sarah really liked Newfoundland, and she says you might return. She liked the vibrant house colours, the icebergs, and Gros Morn Park. She refers to Newfoundland as being just a pretty rock, but she says that the tourist industry wouldn't like her saying that."

Marie looked up directly at Lucas. "You are going to be part of something very important in your line of expertise. It will be a surprise to a great many people. Some very important people but you must be careful."

"Sarah's mother is there and she spends time with her daughter. Sarah uses a lot of energy to help heal family members. I see a cobweb on your face. It's Sarah's energy. She looks deep into your eyes. She can see eye strain. She tells you to look after your eyes.

"She loves to walk. Sarah says she is going to get you a thirty-five-year-old woman to snuggle with and keep warm. Just remember what she told you before. She says she lives in a house like the one down here, but bigger. She loves butterflies. She likes to tease you a bit, moving favourite items around, and then showing you where they are. She loves you very much and will wait for you."

Marie paused to tell Lucas that Sarah looked radiant, and that she had a glow about her.

"She is leaving now but says she is very, very happy. Don't get attached to 'things'. Anything that matters is all in the heart. She blows you a kiss."

Lucas finally relaxed and let all the information sink in. He felt like a wrung-out dishcloth. Looking over at Ann he could see her face all smiles. His tears were very close to the surface, but he was able to control that emotion more than he was able to do following his reading with Rosalie.

"There is another woman coming through. An older woman. Jessica, or Janet. Jessie! Her name is Jessie. This is your mother. She has a lovely smile and curly hair. There is a glow about her also and she is laughing - says it's fun to be talking. She too is around you a lot. She thinks a lot of Sarah. She says the biggest gift you can give to the world is to be generous with love and caring. She is very proud of you and says you will do something great. Your father just left a shed and gives you a big wave. He is building something in the shed. She tells you to stop worrying, and that you have a lot of people watching out for you. She is leaving now. She waves."

Wow! A double whammy! Lucas was all in. 'What a reading,' he thought.

Marie sat back and let her body relax against the back of the chair.

Everyone was speechless and looking at each other. After a few minutes, Marie asked if anyone would like tea, coffee, or wine.

Lucas quickly glanced at Ann and said, "Wine sounds very good right now."

"Well, you two make yourselves comfortable in the living room and I'll bring the wine."

Lucas and Ann returned to their places on the couch, giving each other a warm, tight hug before sitting down. They held hands for a brief time, looking into each other's eyes. It had been another great reading. They liked Marie St-Onge and her approach to hearing the passed souls speak to her. There was something else Lucas wanted to ask Marie about: the afterlife. He hoped she would have something to say about this and would be willing to share her knowledge with him.

Marie brought in a tray which held three wine glasses and a bottle of white wine wrapped in a white cloth. "I only had a Riesling. I hope that is all right."

"It certainly is... Marie. May I call you Marie?" Lucas asked.

70

"Yes, you may. Now, Lucas, you mentioned earlier that you are interested in learning about the afterlife. I know you probably want proof that there is an afterlife, and I can't give you 'proof' as it relates to your understanding of the earthly meaning of proof."

Ann saw that Marie was leaning into Lucas from her chair opposite him, getting very close to his face and never taking her eyes off his, and Ann's beautiful blue-green eyes turned more green than blue the longer she watched Marie's attention.

"First, Lucas, you have to believe that we don't die. Our body dies but our soul, our spirit, lives on. Our souls are made of energy and energy cannot be destroyed. Therefore, where do our souls go? We talk to them, or rather, they talk to us, so we know they exist... somewhere. Or are they forever just floating around in space, doing nothing? Perhaps they *do* lounge around all day on clouds, ala Walt Disney Productions!"

Lucas interrupted Marie. "You advertise as being a firm believer in life after death. Does that not imply that you believe in an afterlife existing somewhere out there where our souls 'live', so to speak?"

"It does just that, Lucas. I *know* there is an afterlife, although I have no concrete proof of its existence. I have been there and know of what I tell you. I have had three near-death experiences. Let me put it this way: we all use 'smart phones'. In fact, we take them for granted. We use all the features, some, too much, and we have no idea how they accomplish all that they can do. And we don't care how they do all that they do. We just accept them. Some will spend hours if not days in a line just to get the newest model. But when it comes to talking about an afterlife, the skeptics and cynics want all kinds of proof. It doesn't count that we have proof of the existence of the soul or spirit, and that they live in the afterlife. NDEs, near-death experiences, are paid little attention. Everyone has an explanation as to what's going on there. I'm sorry, I get quite frustrated when talking about the afterlife. Please excuse me."

"No, no," Lucas said, touching Marie's arm. "I think I know how you feel, and I want to understand as much as I can about all this.

Look, we've kept you long enough. I would appreciate being able to talk to you more about the afterlife on another occasion if I might."

"I would enjoy that too, Lucas. Give me a buzz sometime and we'll get together. Thank you both for coming."

• • • • •

The drive back to Gateway Road was relatively silent as they both reviewed in their minds all the information Marie had brought forth. They exchanged surprised looks and didn't have to say a word. They both knew the meaning of the raised eyebrows. The smiles between them told the rest of the story, Lucas was hooked! Now the lawyer in him would manifest itself and he would have to learn as much as was possible. He knew that Marie St-Onje would be very instrumental.

Ann knew Lucas well enough to know what was going to develop. She knew he would now be like a dog with a bone. She thought back to what Sarah had said, about finding a thirty-five-year-old woman to snuggle with Lucas. She was far from being thirty-five and she felt panicky about losing her relationship with Lucas. How quick would Sarah be with her search? Should she be more forward with Lucas? Solidify her position, so to speak? 'Listen to me go on, just like a school girl!' she admonished herself. She turned toward Lucas and gave him her best come hither look. 'Nothing to lose,' she figured.

Lucas turned into his driveway and thought, 'How strange that you park in a *driveway*, and drive on a *parkway*!' He was anxious to get inside and analyze the events of the afternoon with Ann.

He made drinks and brought them out to the 'war room' where Ann was waiting.

"Well! What are your thoughts on the meeting?" He raised his glass to Ann.

"I thought she was excellent. She certainly seems to have the information to explain what you are looking for. She's been doing readings for some time, I would say. I think she is exactly what you are looking for and she is willing to meet." To herself, Ann thought, '... and she's older than thirty-five.'

"That's the feeling I get too. It will certainly save time, not having to keep searching for a reputable medium. Someone we can trust."

"Lucas, what do you make of her comments, your mother's also, about you and your future? Does any of it make sense?"

"Not right now. Can you find that part on her CD, Ann?"

Ann put the CD in the player and found the appropriate section, after some searching. They watched each other as the CD played.

"It doesn't make any sense right off. I guess it's something you tuck in the back of your mind and hope you recognize it at the right time. I'm going to go nuts until I get another meeting set up. When do you think I should call her?" Lucas asked Ann.

"Try tomorrow. Only way to find out." Ann had a slightly sullen expression. She was becoming slightly uncomfortable around Marie St. Onge.

"Right. Tomorrow. You know, that name, St-Onge, has been bothering me since we first saw it. It rings a bell. I seem to remember it from somewhere. Can I get you another wine?"

"Let's order a pizza, Lucas. We haven't eaten yet. Okay?"

"I like pepperoni."

"I know that."

They enjoyed their pizza in the 'war room', talking well into the night.

"Again, there was that warning, I take it to be a warning, about something happening regarding my work. Do you think it is a warning, Ann?"

"I don't know if it is a dire warning of something bad. Perhaps it's a warning of something occurring related to the law, or the firm. Something along that line. I'm sure you'll recognize it when it happens." She grew serious, and asked, "Lucas, how do you feel now about... death, having had two readings? You must feel differently, more positive maybe? And you *do* realize Sarah still exists. And your parents also. Everyone close to you."

"I tell you Ann, I feel lifted up. The heaviness in my heart is lessening. And yes, now knowing that Sarah is still with me, I have to know more. I want to understand everything now. And there is going to be so much to learn. I feel like I've just awakened from a big sleep. That's a good way to put it. But the fact is, I've only done half the journey. I know grief is a selfish reaction for the most part but isn't it possible and understandable that I can feel joy for Sarah, enjoying her new existence, wherever that may be? Yet because of that very fact, I can feel grief for a whole new reason. I feel now, in some way, that we are farther apart. Instead of it being just me, all alone, which was bad enough, I've now learned that we live in two different worlds. Worlds apart. And her world seems so much better than mine. And it is her world that I want to learn about, that world called the afterlife. Does that make sense to you?"

"Lucas, it makes perfect sense. Will you take me on that journey with you?"

"All the way, Ann. To the end!"

• • • • •

After your death you will be what you were before your birth.
Arthur Schopenhauer

Lucas waited until early afternoon before making the call to Marie St-Onge.

"Hello."

"Hello... Marie." Lucas felt awkward, using her first name. "This is Lucas McNab. I realize this is an imposition but I am so very interested in what you can tell me about the afterlife. Actually, I'm interested in *everything* concerning our souls and the idea that we don't die!"

"Yes, well, this is much sooner than I expected, Lucas. Fortunately, I have a few days to myself. Why don't you come over this afternoon and I'll try to answer what questions you may have. Can you do that?"

"I appreciate you doing this on short notice. Will two be okay?"

"That's fine, Lucas. I'll see you then. Bye."

When Marie answered the door, Lucas presented her with a nice bottle of white wine.

"Just an apology for calling on such short notice," Lucas added.

"Come in, please. Where would you prefer to sit - kitchen or living room?"

Lucas gave a quick, quizzical look at Ann, and said, "I think the kitchen table would be good."

As they positioned themselves around the table, Marie placed her recorder in front of herself. Ann knew, once again, that her note taking wouldn't be necessary.

"Now, Lucas. Where would you like to begin?"

"Well, Marie, I'm new to this whole concept. Ann got me interested in it as a result of the benefit to her in a similar situation. I was a true skeptic until just a few days ago when I had my first reading, and my wife came through and gave me validation. I can't tell you how it changed me. I'm here wanting to learn more about our soul, what happens when we die, what the afterlife is about... everything!"

"Okay, we'll see what we can cover today. First off, let me tell you something of myself. I have been given this gift. I was born with it. As a child I saw people, talked with them, played with the children. My parents were never aware of this taking place as these 'spirits' only came around when I was alone. I learned later that what I experienced was not uncommon in children. Many young kids had what was termed 'imaginary friends', and now it is thought that children experience such things because their minds are still uncluttered, so to speak. They are yet pure. And I'll admit that as I grew older, the images grew fainter and fainter until I fully applied myself to receiving them again. Like any task, the more you practice the better you become.

R . B . B r o w n

"I come by my ability naturally, from my maternal great grand-father who was a seventh son of a seventh son. He was a healer. The story has come down through the family of a man coming to my great grandfather with a goiter on his neck. Supposedly, great grandad rubbed the goiter until beads of perspiration stood out on his forehead, and the goiter was gone!" Marie's pride in her great grandfather was evident. Now turning toward the stove, she said, "I've got the teapot on ready to go. How about a cuppa?"

"That would be lovely," Ann said.

Marie poured three cups and brought them to the table, along with a small pitcher of milk and three spoons.

The tea was good and gave everybody a little time to digest what Marie had told them.

"Now then. A soul. What is a soul and how do we know we have one? You both have had messages from souls or spirits whom you firmly believe to be your loved ones. And Lucas, you are convinced that what you experienced is real, that the spirits I communicated with are your loved ones, correct? What proof do we have of this, in fact? Scientific disciplines certainly don't believe in mediumship because they can't *prove* it by their methods. But that doesn't mean souls don't exist, does it?

"Let's look at the human body. For the most part we take our bodies for granted. But if we look at our body objectively, it is a machine. Take our eyes, for instance. We look at an object with our eyes. There is the pupil. This allows light into the eye. The iris controls the size of the pupil, thereby controlling the amount of light entering the eye. Then there is the lens. This will change shape to allow the eye to focus. There is a light sensitive lining of the eye made up of photosensors, consisting of light sensitive cone and rod cells. Lastly, there is the optic nerve which carries all this collected information to the brain where it is processed and we see the object we were looking at. Just like a machine, or a smartphone.

"Now, machines must have a source of energy. Our bodies are electrical. What we eat supplies the required fuel. If we stop eating, the fuel source dries up, and we die. Except for our soul. The soul is pure energy, and so it cannot be destroyed. What happens to it? Science explains it away by saying it just floats away, somewhere in the atmosphere. What happens is that when you die, your soul is no longer confined by a physical body. You, the soul, becomes part of the afterlife. You can fly! I often compare it to the Peter Pan movie. Remember that?"

Marie continued. "As well as shedding the human body, all pain, all negativity is gone, but all the good from your stay on Earth remains with your soul." She paused. "Now, a little stretch will do us good about now. I'll get us something cold to drink."

Lucas and Ann had a blank stare in their eyes. Marie had provided them with a great deal of information to absorb all at once. They looked at each other. Their words wouldn't come, but Ann knew Lucas was excited over what Marie had told them.

Marie returned with glasses of iced tea.

"What you have been saying, Marie, is a lot to take in, all at one time. I am simply astounded. You explained it so well."

"Well, I know it goes against everything you were probably brought up to believe, but it makes so much sense. Nothing about mediumship goes against what the Bible has to say. In fact, the scriptures back up what is written about souls. So, I don't understand how the church, Western orthodoxy, can come out so vehemently opposed to what we do."

"I would agree with you on that," said Ann.

"All right, Lucas. Next comes the afterlife, as we term it. From my experiences, and I've had a few, I define the afterlife as a parallel universe to the one we live in here on Earth. But everything is much more intense. The colours are vibrant, the flowers are huge and colourful, as are the birds and butterflies. Beautiful green grass and walkways everywhere. A deep blue sky with puffy white and pink clouds. It is simply wonderful. All of this is a result of increased vibrations. There are buildings that house libraries, study halls, and other rooms for different activities. Lucas, have you ever seen the Sagrada Familia in Barcelona?" Lucas shook his head."Well, the buildings I have seen look quite a bit like that."

Marie continued."Some people leave suddenly and other people can take a long time. It has all been laid out for you: when you are born, and when you die. And grief is all part of this process. Grief will be experienced worldwide, although death is accepted in different ways. In some societies death becomes a celebration, a party, for a short while. But people tend to hold on to grief for selfish reasons."

Lucas interrupted. "Excuse me, Marie, but isn't it natural to be happy, for a better word, for the person who has passed, but grieve for being left alone and the loss that is experienced? Is that being selfish?"

"You have a valid point, but unless you *believe* the soul passes to the afterlife, you really have nothing to be happy about, unless the person that has passed was in great pain or difficulty. Your grief then never gets past the grave. Does that make sense?"

Lucas nodded.

"In fact, the soul, having reached the astral plane, doesn't care a fig about their outer shell, the body. They forget about it completely. They don't care what happens to it."

Lucas had another question. "You talk about the soul, which we can't see. What form, if any, does the soul take on after crossing over?"

"Everything and everybody has a solid form. They keep the body they occupied here, but they can be any age they choose. Everything is real, Lucas. As I mentioned earlier, it is like a parallel 'world'. Wonderful forests, mountains, lakes, rivers, just like here, only much brighter and more intense."

Lucas was hesitant about his next question. "Will it be possible to, say... hold hands?"

"Yes, Lucas."

"...and hug, and hold a person, and even... kiss?"

"Yes, yes, and yes, Lucas. It will all be the same, but so much better," explained Marie.

"There is much to do on that astral plane. There are huge buildings where you can attend classes on anything. You can work with other souls helping them leave their earthly plane; you can help souls that will be returning to earthly bodies; there are counsellors and healers; you might even become a spirit guide. You can study and learn to do things you were not able to do here on Earth such as learning to play the guitar. Perhaps you always wanted to be an actor. That can be done in the afterlife. You can fly like the wind, be in two places at the same time. You can even travel to other galaxies. And much more.

"I must add that what you do with your life while on Earth has a bearing on your acceptance into the afterlife. You *will* be judged as to what level of the afterlife you will be 'assigned'. Now you can understand why science scoffs at such an idea, and to some extent, the church also.

"Lucas, have I answered your questions? That's about all I can tell you without going into details that wouldn't necessarily help you. I must say, I feel so sorry for those who see nothing beyond the grave. What is their purpose here on Earth? Of course, we are all brought up with orthodoxy drummed into our heads, and we've been lied to all our life. For centuries. As children we had it pounded into our heads about a vindictive God who will punish you for doing bad things. We were scared silly. It's a wonder there are any churchgoers left! Practically every civilization now and throughout history has had a similar belief as I've outlined today. Here is something to think about: it doesn't matter where you live, your skin colour, or your religious belief. Every person on this Earth will experience some variation of what I have laid out. The sad part is this: if you have not prepared yourself by educating yourself as to what takes place when you die, you are in for a very frightening transformation. There, I've stopped!" Marie, eyes wide open, smiled at the couple as she stood up.

"I want to pay you for this meeting, Marie. Tell me."

"No charge for this, Lucas. It means a lot to me to have a discourse from time to time. And I have a good feeling that I will see you again. I couldn't help but read you a little, psychically, and I see a challenge for you in the near future. I couldn't determine just what that challenge will be, but it appeared in a good light."

"We thank you so much for this. It has been a most enjoyable experience. We wish you all the very best, and we could well be in touch! Take care, Marie." Lucas gave a slight wave on leaving.

• • • • •

They drove back to the city, neither saying much. Both were deep on thought. For Ann, a long-time believer, being with Lucas these past days and experiencing the enlightenment again was exciting. The hurtful memories of losing Robert were gone now. The future was what mattered, and the exciting afterlife. Lucas was becoming a bigger part of her future, it seemed, and she was all right with that, wherever it took her.

Lucas broke their reverie. "Let's grab a bite to eat someplace."

"And clear our heads!" Ann added.

They drove down Hollis and found a parking place near the Bluenose ll restaurant. They sat in a booth next to the street and placed their orders with the waiter. The session with Marie St-Onge had given them much to think about.

"Did Marie help you understand what's happening with our life and death, Lucas?" Marie asked gently.

Lucas sat looking out at the street. He didn't say anything for a few minutes. His thoughts were on what Marie had said about becoming a person again and being able to hold and kiss Sarah again. He hoped with all his heart that she was right. He finally turned to face Ann. He took her hand and squeezed it slightly. He needed contact with a solid form. He needed a human touch, something he understood. Even though he believed in everything Marie had told him, her clarity of definitions had raised his conscience to a new level and left him with even more questions.

"Sorry, Ann. Didn't mean to ignore you. I've got so many thoughts running around in my head right now. We've got a lot to talk about. Right?"

They ate their meals and returned to Gateway by early evening. Lucas purposely opened the garage door and drove the Equinox in under cover, looking at Sarah's Miata all the while. He was somewhat surprised and relieved that it didn't affect him in the usual way. He was making progress.

Ann went to the kitchen. "Shall I put on some coffee?"

"I think so," replied Lucas, as he hung up their coats in the entry closet. "I'll check the 'war room' and make a fire," he chuckled.

Ann soon joined him with the coffee and made herself comfortable in the leather chair. She could tell by his expression that he had been thinking seriously about the session with Marie.

"Thanks, Ann. You know, I've been trying to picture what implications and ramifications all this could cause societies worldwide. The results would be quite staggering when you put it in perspective. Think about the consequences. It would affect the undertaking profession to a great extent. And what pandemonium in the law courts! There would have to be monumental changes to the judiciary world-wide, no doubt!"

"And churches. If they survived, they would have to change their approach of delivering their messages. Their congregations, if they still had any, would be more enlightened than ever," Ann added.

Lucas responded, "Remember what Sarah said when we had the reading with Rosalie? She said… I can't remember exactly, but it was something about material things; that they don't mean anything. Just what's in the heart is what matters. Remember that, Ann? It was in Marie's reading too. In that case, trade with China would dry up, a good thing I would say. And Wal-Mart wouldn't be able to purchase product. Another good thing! You could go on and on. But all of it would be for the better. Mind you, there are many societies throughout the world who are living, have *been* living this way for eons. You know them, Ann. They're the peoples we've been taught to refer to as 'backward'!"

"I agree with you, Lucas, but you can't change the world overnight. Marie is correct in saying more and more people throughout the world are questioning our values. They're realizing all the lies we've been fed for centuries and they're looking for a better way. It will be slow and it will be small, but it is a beginning."

"Ah, you're right, Ann. Here I am off on another tangent. Let's hit the sack. I have no idea what we'll do tomorrow, but I'm sure events will unfold as they should. Right?"

"Right. Having anything stronger than coffee before you turn in?"

"Now, there. A small dram might help me to sleep. How about you?"

"Do you know, as a celebratory occasion, I am going to try a scotch too!"

"Well, well! This *will* be a day to remember. I applaud your decision and welcome you to the club."

Bringing out a bottle of twelve year single malt, Lucas poured two small glasses. He passed one to Ann.

"Now, this is sipping stuff. Introduce yourself to it slowly. Take in the mild, peaty aroma. Take a sip and roll it around the tongue, warming it up. That's it. Now let it glide down the throat and feel its warming effect."

Ann followed his instructions and reacted with a shudder, a wry mouth, and tears in her eyes.

"Oh... oh, Lucas. How can you drink that stuff? It tastes horrible!"

"It *is* an acquired taste, I grant you. Brave girl for even trying," he said kindly, and he gave her a hug. "So, it's off to bed we go then. Will see you in the morning. 'Nite, Ann."

"Good night, Lucas. Have a good sleep," and she blew him a kiss from the stairway.

• • • • •

The next morning, over coffee, they discussed the explanations Marie had given them.

"Marie made excellent sense regarding the soul and the afterlife, but I want to go deeper into each one," exclaimed Lucas. "I think she kept it simple because we were new at it all, and she purposely didn't want to overwhelm us with all the technical and paranormal info. But that's what I want to learn more about."

"Well, we know how to research, don't we? At least I do." Ann laughed. "We can start right here, on your computer. Right?"

"Right. Where do we start?"

"Make a list of topics you're interested in."

"I've got a pretty good list in my head. Let's start with the soul."

Ann had moved to the computer in the small room just off the dining area. She typed in 'soul' and waited while the computer searched. She ran the cursor down the first page, searching for a site that looked promising. It quickly became obvious that there was a plethora of soul sites.

"Here's one that states that our souls are connected to our hearts. It mentions vibrations, and that what talents we have now are accumulated from past lives. We have to access our soul, listen to it, and it will provide a meaningful life. What do you think?"

Lucas shrugged his shoulders and motioned Ann to try another site.

"Look here. It says that 'soul' comes from Old English, with various meanings: *life, **spirit**, being.* Here's another definition of soul, Lucas. 'The *spirit* or essence of a person, usually thought to consist of one's thoughts and personality.' Listen to this! *'Often believed to live on after a person's death'*!"

It was starting to come together for Lucas.

"Listen to this one." Ann proceeded to read the text aloud, even as Lucas was reading it silently.

"Okay. It starts out by saying that you choose your missions or assignments as a spirit and the clues as to what these assignments are manifest themselves through your earthly desires. Through these missions your chief aim is to bring joy, peace, and love to your part of the Earth. Also, as an infinite soul, you have kept special talents from past lives. These you can apply to the task of fulfilling your assignments."

Ann took a swallow of coffee, looked at Lucas who was still reading, and continued.

"You must trust yourself to follow what you enjoy the most. Follow your heart, which, in effect, is your soul. The most common time for heart attacks is early Monday morning. Coincidence? Or are they job-related?

"We are all role-playing, here on Earth - father, husband, friend, worker, church member, and so on. We must fulfil our role fully, to the very best of our ability. A well-known doctor and spiritualist has put it this way: 'If you knew you would not fail, how would you live your life? By doing this you will become aware of what your soul is asking of you. By committing to your soul's contract, you will connect with the purpose and joy of your birthright.'"

Both sat back, looked at each other, and let out a long sigh.

"That was all pretty deep," Ann said.

"But it all makes sense," added Lucas. "Think of the numerous expressions that include the heart and the soul. The song 'Heart and Soul', for example. The expression, 'he has a good heart.'"

"'He's a kind soul'," added Ann. "And you often hear something like, 'Fifty souls were lost at sea...', not fifty bodies. But then again, you do hear 'three bodies were found, blah, blah'."

"When it's said, 'he has a black heart', or 'he has no heart', are they actually referring to that person's soul?" Lucas wondered.

"'You've Got Me Body and Soul!" exclaimed Ann excitedly. "Soul music!"

"'O Soul Mio'," shouted Lucas, and they both broke out laughing.

They were getting tired and giddy over the sheer concentration the research was taking. They had been at it for hours.

"Time for a break." Lucas stood up and stretched.

"You got that right!" Ann did the same.

"What about a walk? Clear our heads and get some so-called 'fresh air'?"

"That's a great idea, Lucas. Let's go."

They took a leisurely stroll down Gateway, arm in arm. They were quiet, listening to a few birds and enjoying the good weather on this particular morning.

Lucas broke their reverie. "There are lots of references to the spirit too, eh. Like 'team spirit', 'where's your spirit?', 'it was a spirited race'. When was the term first used? And where did it originate? It doesn't have the same meaning as 'soul'. I mean, the two aren't interchangeable, are they? Yet mediums use them both in the same breath. I don't get it."

"Well, we'll research that when we get back home."

They both felt refreshed after the walk. Ann returned to the computer while Lucas perked another pot of coffee.

"Listen to this, Lucas: 'Spirit: the non-physical part of a person which is the seat of emotions and character...' the *soul*! And here it states that spirit is from Old English based on the Latin *spiritus*, which translates to *breath*."

"Hold on there, I'm coming. Here's your coffee. Now let me see this."

"Here. The plural is given as *'the collective souls of man'.* The various translations include *soul*. That's all pretty definitive, Lucas. The soul and the spirit are the same thing."

"That pretty well settles one concern I had. Now, the difficult one. The afterlife. I believe the best we can do to answer this is to come to as positive a conclusion as is possible. Don't you think, Ann? It appears that man has been searching for the truth about an afterlife since time immemorial - with no concrete answers. This doesn't auger well for our attempt!" Lucas joked.

"Let's go back over your readings," suggested Ann. "The afterlife was mentioned by both Rosalie and Marie. We can start there."

"That will be a good start, and we might pick up some valuable leads too," Lucas agreed.

Ann spread her notes from Rosalie's reading over the table. "You asked her if she had seen the afterlife. Remember, Lucas? She stared out the window for a time before she answered you, almost like she was seeing it all again in her mind. She said it was simply beautiful and there was a beautiful light everywhere making everything bright. She said she wanted to go there. I take from her words that she wanted to stay. She spoke of the flowers being so big and pretty. She saw her husband but he looked younger. That's it. Oh, wait. While Sarah was coming through, at one point she compared being there like being on holiday."

"I remember that. One thing about Rosalie, Ann: you can trust what she tells you. She is telling you just what she saw. Let's find out if Marie's information squares with Rosalie's. Is the CD right there?"

"I've got it. Here."

Lucas loaded it in the CD deck and started searching for the relevant part of Marie's reading.

"Found it. Ann, please make notes of what she says," Lucas requested.

They listened intently as Marie began. She had three near-death experiences, NDEs she called them. She saw the afterlife each time. Saw what she called a parallel universe to ours. Everything more intense. Vibrant colours everywhere - flowers, birds, butterflies, grass. Paths were everywhere. Beautiful forests and mountains. Deep blue sky with fluffy pink and white clouds. Everything is real and has a solid form. All created by increase in vibrations.

"Whatever that means," added Ann. They listened for a few more minutes, until Ann said, "There. She brings up that Sagrada Familia in Barcelona. Stop the CD, Lucas. We'll look that up."

When they found it, they were shocked! It looked like it belonged on another planet.

"Wow! Would you look at that. It fits right in with the descriptions of the afterlife we've been told about. Designed and constructed by Antoni Gaudi, 1852-1926. It's not finished yet! In 2010 it was one-half completed. They think it will be finished in 2026, one hundred years after his death. That's just amazing! It's the largest unfinished cathedral in the world!"

They continued playing Marie's CD, and Ann continued reading from her notes.

"She talked about being able to learn new things - things you always wanted to do: play the guitar, write books, teach. You can fly like the wind. Be in two places at once. Visit other galaxies. Again, she stressed the point about being judged by your life here on Earth. And that's about it, Lucas."

Lucas turned the player off and sat back with a look of disbelief. He had difficulty relating to all he had heard. He felt isolated. The information they had found made Lucas feel farther away from Sarah. They truly were in two different worlds.

"What's next, chief?" Ann asked.

Lucas turned to Ann with a questioning look. "Ann, I've got to get away from all this for a while. Would you come with me and travel for a few days? We'll just go. The Valley perhaps. Visit some wineries. What do you say?"

Ann's heart started beating a little faster. She thought, 'I hope I'm not blushing.' After a few seconds she responded, "Actually, Lucas, I think it is a great idea, and I would love to go with you."

"All right, then. Lets head to the 'war room' and we'll christen our trip. Wine for the lady, scotch for me." Lucas felt better, returning to Earth.

· · · · ·

After a light breakfast, they drove out the Bedford Highway and took the 101 turn off at Lower Sackville, heading for Windsor. It was an excellent highway and would get them to Avondale in a short time.

"Our first stop on this wine tour will be the Avondale Sky Winery, Ann. It's a beautiful spot on the St Croix River. They brought a church from Walton to here, by barge, if you can imagine. That's their wine tasting centre now. I'm not familiar with their wines, but we'll try a few. Not too early in the morning for you, is it?"

"My good man, it is *never* too early for me!" Ooops!

They soon arrived at the winery and made their way to the beautiful old church. They sampled a few of the wines and thought them quite good, Ann being the connoisseur. They decide on 2012 Pinot Noir and bought three bottles.

"What a wonderful location, Lucas!"

"Isn't it, though. I was reading in there that tides can reach forty-three feet! That's some tide!"

As they drove back to the highway, Lucas asked, "How about we stop in Windsor and get something to eat?"

"Sounds like a good idea. Got anything in mind?"

"I've been to the Spitfire Arms with good results. It had a fire a while back. Don't know if they had to change location or not. Want to give it a try?"

"Anything you say. You're my tour guide on this trip."

Lucas drove up Water Street and saw the Spitfire Arms where it used to be. He turned left and found a spot in a small parking lot. They walked across the street to the Arms. Inside, they decided to sit at the English style bar, a large, square hardwood structure with a friendly host. They ate light. Lucas ordered the Spitfire Clubhouse with hand-cut chips and Ann had the spinach salad. Both had a Principal draft.

They were taken with the decor and explored the room while waiting for their orders. On one wall was a large colourful poster stating: '10th happiest place in Canada - Expedia'.

"I just bet it is on a Friday night." Lucas chuckled.

After lunch, they took a short walk to stretch their legs. They had parked beside a flower shop, and Lucas hurried in. He asked for one red rose. Jennifer, the owner, selected a beautiful, large, deep red one, removed the thorns, and passed it to him. Returning to the car, he opened the passenger side door and presented the rose to Ann.

Ann took the rose and looked into Lucas' eyes. "Thank you," was all she said. Lucas took her hand and softly kissed it. And this time Ann didn't care if she blushed.

"Next stop, Sainte-Famille Winery."

"Where is it, Lucas?"

"Falmouth, just across the river. It's one of the original three wineries in the province, I believe."

Very soon, Lucas turned up a rather steep driveway to the winery. It wasn't a large winery but they hosted many events throughout the year. They sampled a few wines and bought several bottles.

They left Sainte-Famille and found their way back to the 101, the Harvest Highway. Lucas turned off at the Grand Pré exit, passing the Just Us Coffee and Tea House.

"Just ahead there's a little store we should stop at called the Tangled Garden. They make their own jellies and jams. It is gourmet stuff. We should pick up some jam, don't you think?" Lucas suggested.

"Sure. Let's," Ann quickly agreed.

"The only thing missing is parking space." Lucas pulled in and parked, barely off the road.

They had difficulty deciding on what jams they would buy, as it was such an unusual variety. They finally settled on Raspberry Lavender jam and Ginger Lime Thyme jelly.

"Oh, I can't wait to get home to try them," Ann smiled in anticipation.

As they drove on, Lucas faced a dilemma that he had thought about since planning this trip. Namely, where will they sleep, and more importantly, *how* will they sleep? He had made little overtures to Ann trying to tell her he cared for her, and she seemed to indicate that she cared for him too. This was all so new to him, but he craved the naked touch of a woman's body. He longed for the warmth, the cuddling. But... Ann. Their friendship went way back and it just didn't seem right. He had considered the Olde Lantern Inn where he and Sarah had often stayed, but it just didn't seem like the right place. They had enjoyed that B&B and the proximity to the winery, but it was too early in the season to really enjoy the great meals there.

As he approached the Evangeline Motel, he quickly decided a motel would be the best choice for them. Although he disliked the association that went with a motel, it gave them options.

"Let's see if we can get rooms?" he stressed the plural. "Doesn't look too bad and we can eat here too. What do you say, Ann?"

"It looks all right to me. We just need a place to sleep." Ann's mind was trying to calculate the situations that could present themselves.

Lucas was able to get two adjoining rooms, and after storing their goods and belongings they visited the restaurant for coffee and to look over their menu.

"It's always satisfying to find some sort of shelter when you're traveling, isn't it?" Ann asked.

"It really is. Sarah and I have been caught like that a few times, and I've had to drive many more miles searching, and usually paying top dollar when we finally found something."

"So, what have you lined up for us next, Lucas?" Ann asked.

"There are a couple of wineries close by we should visit. One, the Grand Pré Winery, is just up the road. Then farther on, there's the Lightfoot and Wolfville Vineyards."

"Well then, what are we waiting for? Let's go, driver!"

They parked in the lot just off the road at the Grand Pré Winery and walked up the rather steep incline to the gift shop. Lucas got

Ann to peer into the dining area, and he pointed out the beautiful woodwork.

"Too bad it's not open. Excellent meals. You know, we've come at a really bad time to visit the wineries. They're half-closed up this time of year. We'll come back in the fall."

They sampled more wine and bought four bottles of the Tidal Bay. Returning to the Equinox, Lucas pulled out an equipment bag stuffed with towels.

"What in the world are you going to do with that?"

"That, my girl, is going to hold our wine, protected with the towels. See? My mother didn't raise no idjits!"

"Well, now. Ain't you jest the smartest little non-idjit!" Ann teased. They laughed as they climbed into the vehicle.

"Next stop, Lightfoot and Wolfville Vineyards, just up the road."

They parked in front of the large brown, barn-like building. There were hardly any visitors around. They entered and proceeded to the long tasting bar. There were two men explaining the wines to a small group of five people. Lucas and Ann decided on the Ancienne Pinot Noir.

"I do believe we have enough wine to get us through to spring, now," Lucas quipped as he zipped up the bag. He also pulled the cover over the top to hide everything from prying eyes.

"We should plan on eating soon, Lucas. Any ideas on that?" Ann was getting hungry.

"Not really. Let's just drive through Wolfville and see what they've got," Lucas said.

They decided on Paddy's Brew Pub and Rosie's Restaurant. Lucas had steak and Ann had the scallops.

Since daylight was fading they decided to call it a day, and they headed back to the motel.

• • • • •

Lucas decided to freshen up and give Ann time to do the same. He took the wine he had brought in from the car and put in the sink with cold water to chill it. He sat back in the chair and contemplated the day. More importantly, the *night*! When he had needed help in the past, he would sing out to Sarah, 'help me Rhonda, help, help me Rhonda!' And he softly sang that plea again. 'Help me Sarah...'! He needed this change of pace. All the talk of other worlds was disturbing to him. Ignorance was *definitely* bliss! He was nearly asleep in the chair when he heard tapping on the door. He rubbed his eyes, stood up, and opened the door. It was Ann, with a bottle of wine! She was way ahead of him.

"Why, hello there. Peddling wine, are we? I'll take a bottle and do come in. I'll get glasses."

Ann placed the bottle on the small table and sat on the edge of the bed. Lucas brought two rather large glasses from the bathroom and removed the protective wrapping. He opened the wine and poured a good measure in each glass, passing one to Ann.

"Here's to our get-away. May it last forever!" Lucas leaned in to Ann to clink her glass.

"Here, here!" Ann cheered.

"But, you know, I can't stop thinking about all we've learned about the paranormal, if that's the proper term. Can you?" Lucas asked.

"I guess it's been in the back of my mind too, Lucas. Everything we've learned or been told is really mind-bending. It is truly astounding. How could you forget it?"

Lucas took a deep breath and began. "I want you to think about what I'm going to say. You will easily relate to my premise. Listen now. We agree that the body is just a means of transportation for the soul, correct? And when the body dies, the soul lives on, right?

After death, the body means nothing. It is just a shell, of no use. Now, the soul passes on to the afterlife, and we both have pretty good proof of that happening. Agreed? There is no concrete scientific proof that this is what happens, but it is becoming more and more acceptable thinking as more and more people open up their minds to the distinct possibility, plus the many, many 'eye witness' testimonials from the NDEs.

"Now, here's what bothers me, and it does so primarily because I am a trial lawyer. If all I've just said is true," Lucas looked hard at Ann, getting her full attention, "if that is true... can there really be such a crime as murder?"

Ann looked completely stunned. Lucas looked intently in her eyes, waiting for her first words. Both were silent for a few minutes. Each finally took a large swallow of wine.

"My God, Lucas! Could you be right? Do you know what that would do to the whole judiciary system? The effect it would have on society? The possible chaos?" Ann burst out.

"I know, I know. Don't think I haven't considered all those ram-ifications and what they would mean. We talked about the effects just the other day. Nonetheless, if it were true, couldn't it be used as a defence? *Shouldn't* it be used as a defence? I don't mean for the accused to get off scot-free, mind. But some other charge could be created, surely. Lord, North America creates more laws than the rest of the world, now."

"Let's create a scenario," suggested Ann, trying to understand.

"Okay. Here's one. A young couple out driving. He's under the influence of something or other and is driving too fast. He leaves the road, hits a tree, his passenger dies - correction, his passenger's *body* dies - but we know her soul lives. He survives and is charged as being responsible for her 'death'. But, but, he only was responsible for 'killing' the body, because his girlfriend still lives. Her soul, her personality lives on, perhaps eventually in another body. What do you think?"

"You would have a helluva time even introducing that defence to the court. I'm not saying you're wrong Lucas, but it's so, so... radical! You would have to convert the minds of everyone involved. That means completely changing their religious beliefs. It could never happen. You'd be laughed out of court. And what about the accused? You would have to convince him too. I'm pretty sure he'd be asking for another lawyer. Whatever made you think of this, Lucas?" Ann asked.

"I don't know, Ann. I was rolling around some thoughts and this just popped up. It made sense to me and I'll bet you every psychic, every medium, would see it too. I agree with every point you bring up without argument, but you must agree on one thing: it has merit. You are so right about closed minds though." Lucas affirmed.

Lucas retrieved the wine from the bathroom sink and refilled their glasses. Ann was now looking quite relaxed, sitting with her back against the headboard of the bed.

Lucas delved further into the topic. "Imagine how different this old world would be if all the so-called leaders believed as we believe - that there is something beautiful beyond the grave, but to get there, your life, what you have done to spread love and peace here on Earth, will be judged. That all the crimes and hateful actions you are responsible for don't end with death but are carried with you to the afterlife where you are answerable to a higher power. I firmly believe that the evil among us think, 'Hey, what have I got to worry about? When I die it'll be all over so I don't care. I can do what I want.' I would love to see their faces when they reach the other side, *if* they reach the other side."

He paced around the room as he talked. Not hearing any comments from Ann, he looked over at the bed and saw her, sound asleep. 'Well now, isn't that something!' He removed her shoes, rearranged the pillows under her head, reached across her body, and pulled the comforter over her. As he watched her breathing he realized how much she meant to him, and how grateful he was to have a friend like her. He gave a deep breath, turned, and made his way to her room and her bed.

• • • • •

Sunlight was laying silently across the foot of the bed when Lucas rubbed his eyes and greeted the day. As his feet found the floor and he saw he was still in his clothes, the previous night came quickly into focus. He slipped into his shoes and went to the bathroom, where he splashed cold water on his face, ran his fingers through his rumpled hair, and noticed how tired and old he looked. He opened his door and peeked in. Ann was still in his bed. He went over and gently shook her shoulder.

"Ann, Ann. Wake up, love. Wakey, wakey."

Ann slowly opened her eyes, stretched, and looked questioningly at Lucas then around the room.

In a gravelly voice she said, "What are you doing here? Where am I? Why am I still dressed?"

Lucas explained the night's developments and Ann apologized profusely.

"Listen, go get cleaned up. Take a shower as I'm going to, and we'll go have something to eat," Lucas suggested.

They took a table by the window, discovered they were famished, and ordered the full breakfast, starting with two large coffees. Neither spoke about the previous night. Lucas noticed Ann was avoiding looking at him, and the talk was truly small. Finally, Lucas mentioned driving up to the Look Off. Ann thought that would be nice. They finished their meal, packed up the vehicle, and headed to Wolfville where the road led to Port Williams and Blomidon. As they arrived at the little roadside stop, the sky was clear and bright without a chemtrail in sight. They walked over to the fence and looked out over the valley.

"Oh, Lucas, it is so beautiful!" Ann exclaimed.

"Apparently you can see five counties on a clear day like this. It's a popular spot. As a kid I remember a trip up here was quite often a family excursion. Pack a picnic lunch, bring a couple of blankets to lay on the ground. You could go right to the edge back then. Now, the government says we don't have the brains to take care of ourselves and they put up a fence. Maybe they're right in that thinking," Lucas reflected.

"That sounds like so much fun. I wish we could go back to those times, Lucas."

"So do I, Ann, so do I!"

Lucas moved closer to Ann and placed his arm around her shoulder. She laid her head against him, and they were content with each other.

"Lucas, thank you for being the gentleman I knew you to be, last night. And I apologize for falling asleep as you were talking." She smiled up at him, and he gave her a kiss on the forehead.

Lucas whispered in her ear, "I knew you weren't thirty-five." And they both laughed.

They left Blomiden and headed back to the town. Lucas turned on the car stereo and found a CBC station. The news was just beginning. He turned up the volume. They hadn't heard any news for several days now. The world news wasn't of much interest to either one of them, but then came Maritime news.

'Halifax police are saying a body has been discovered at the park bandstand. Although early in their investigation, it is treated as a murder. The victim appears to be a street person, male, in his sixties. No weapon has been found and no signs of a struggle. The police have a suspect in custody but there is nothing further being given out. We will bring you up-to-date as we learn more.'

"It seems like there's a murder every single day, doesn't it?" Lucas turned down the volume of the radio.

"It really does," said Ann.

"Well, where to now? Hungry? I was thinking of taking the road from Kentville to Chester. Want to do that? There won't be many places to eat along the way so maybe we'll get something in Kentville."

"That's all fine with me, Lucas. Do you know any places in Kentville?" she asked.

"Oh, we'll find something."

It was a short trip back to Wolfville. There was the usual steady, stream of traffic going through New Minas. There were lots of places to eat, but nothing caught Lucas' interest. They followed the road into Kentville and the one-way lane turning left on Webster Street. Another left at traffic lights brought Paddy's Brew Pub to their attention. Lucas found a parking space close by.

"Now, isn't that confusing? Those one-way streets must drive tourists around the bend! No wonder the town isn't as busy as it used to be," Lucas noted. He took Ann's arm and they both ran across the street to the pub, in between the traffic.

Inside they found the usual pub atmosphere. Subdued lighting, the bar, waiters scurrying around, local rummies at tables they think they own, the occasional rough language, everything that makes a pub, a pub!

They found a corner booth in a quieter part, sat down, and observed their surroundings. Soon, a bouncy, young girl came with menus and a pitcher of water. She was full of personality and made them feel welcome. She asked if they wanted something to drink, and Lucas asked for her recommendations. She told them the blueberry beer was very popular. Blueberry beer! Lucas couldn't imagine anything more disgusting! However, Ann was intrigued enough to try it. Lucas ordered Chivas Regal on the rocks.

After looking over the menu, Ann chose the fish cakes and Lucas decided on scallops. They were enjoying the change from the city. Neither had traveled much in several years. It didn't seem that long to Lucas, until he started to count the time from Sarah's onset of dementia and realized that it had been years. He could only remember her progression in fits and starts now.

But here they were, he and Ann, having a pretty good little vacation. One he felt he deserved, but guilt still haunted him.

Little Miss Congeniality arrived with their drink order and told them their meals would be right along. Ann timidly tasted her blueberry beer, and her eyes opened wide in surprise.

"Oh, Lucas, this is good. Try some."

Lucas tried to beg off but Ann was persistent, so he took a small sip.

"Well, now that's not bad at all. Who would have guessed? Beer from blueberries! That's got to be doubly good for you."

The girl came back and placed their dishes on the table. "Enjoy."

The food was good and they indulged in a bit of people-watching. Lucas left a good tip for the little waitress, and they were soon on the road again. He found Chester Avenue and followed it out to and over the Harvest Highway.

"See if you can pick up any news on that murder in Halifax, Ann, please," Lucas requested.

Ann searched until she found a clear CBC signal. "It will soon be on the hour. We should hear something more by now. Why are you so interested? You don't think Wiff Brannigan would be interested in something like this, do you?"

"No way. There ain't no money in this deal!"

'...and now local news. Police have released more on the murder that occurred last night at the Public Gardens...'

"Turn it up, Ann."

'...The victim has been identified as Charles Conlon of no fixed address. He was also known as Chuck or Chook Conlon. He is believed to be in his sixties. Cause of death is not known at this time, but liquor is involved. An autopsy has been ordered. The accused is Joseph Simpson of no known address, but he is known on the street to have been seen with Conlon. Simpson is thought to be in his seventies. Simpson turned himself in to the police early this morning. In other news...'

They drove along in silence, each with their own thoughts. They were each trying to remember something from the recent past. What was it? It seemed as if the news of the murder stirred an ember in their minds, but they couldn't quite fan it into a flame.

Then, suddenly, Ann sat bolt upright. "Lucas! Remember your readings with Rosalie? When she asked you if you knew a Charles, or a Chuck? Remember? Both those names were just there... In the newscast... Charles and Chuck!"

"By damn, you're right. I *do* remember that. You don't suppose..." He retreated to his thoughts. Was there a connection to be found amidst all this? Or was it just a coincidence? They drove on for miles, neither speaking because there was nothing to be said. But each mind was working overtime, looking for a clue to give meaning to these events unfolding before them. Lucas reached for Ann's hand, partly to break into her reverie but also to touch something real. Smiling, she turned to him and covered his hand with hers.

"Let's go in to Chester and Mahone Bay. This could be our last trip together for a while so let's do it," Lucas said.

"You're right about the trip so let's go," Ann agreed.

The road from Kentville continued to Chester Basin. Lucas loved the coast of his province, and he and Sarah hadn't seen much of it. He drove slowly, taking in the ice-free shoreline with gentle waves breaking slowly, peacefully. Ann leaned over toward his side to see. Lucas pushed himself back to make room for her and his view now took in Ann's face. She felt his gaze, turned, raised her head and gently kissed him. He closed his eyes for a second as she closed hers and felt himself melting into the seat. He watched her as she returned to her side. He nearly stopped the car to regain his senses. Ann looked away, somewhat embarrassed, but this time she *knew* she wasn't blushing.

They continued down the coast, each looking out their side. Lucas was confused. Ann's kiss had certainly taken his mind away from Charles What's-his-name and given him a whole new interest.

"Say, we could stop at Oak Island and throw some money in the pit. It'll be the only 'treasure' anybody will ever find. They do have tours if you're interested, Ann."

"Noooo. I don't think so. I've seen enough of that island on the tube. They've been working that old saw for years. They're welcome to anything they find."

Lucas found a small viewing turn-off and drove in. They sat silently, watching the movement of the sea. The water looked cold and uninviting. Time passed, with both deep in their thoughts. Lucas felt that the events of the day were rushing at him. He felt unable to pick and choose. Things were getting in each other's way. He had to untangle them. Each was important to him.

"Ann, let's get something to eat and we'll head back to the city. Okay?" Lucas asked.

"Yes, I think we should," Ann agreed.

Lucas drove on to Mahone Bay, evaluating each eating place as he passed. Then, right in the village, he saw Rebecca's Restaurant. He parked nearby and they went in. The interior was delightful. Timbered ceilings, lots of brick and stone, light and airy, and with a little bar as you entered. They turned right and took the last booth. They weren't that hungry but realized this would be their supper. They both ordered pan seared haddock served with a winter salad and a bottle of Benjamin Bridge Tidal Bay.

When they finished eating and the dishes were cleared away, there was some small talk about the meal and what a discovery Rebecca's was, each making every effort to keep the conversation light and impersonal. Lucas eventually brought them back to reality by referring to the recent murder.

"I've been thinking and thinking about that murder and everything associated with it, however little that is right now, and I have a strong feeling that I must get involved. I'm beginning to understand Rosalie's reading, you know, about the 'Charles' thing. I can't just ignore that. It won't go away. And then there's the part inferring a career change in late spring. Marie read something along these lines too. We'll check your notes when we get back. Dear Ann, don't be too shocked about what I'm about to say." Lucas refilled their glasses before continuing.

"...I want to defend the man accused of the murder." He looked for some tell-tale change in Ann's countenance and saw none.

"I want to introduce a defence based on what we have learned about death and dying, the soul, the afterlife... everything."

"Is this fair to the accused? You have the proverbial snowball's chance of winning on those grounds. You know that, don't you?" Ann spoke seriously.

"Well, let's look at the facts regarding the accused. He is homeless, living on the street. Jail is probably the best place for him. He will think of it as a vacation! Warm bed every night. Lots of food. He can wash himself, and two, best of all, he won't have to belittle himself anymore by begging. Tell me what's wrong with that? If I fail in defending him, how can I hurt him? That's the life waiting for him, and at his age it is, without a doubt, the best thing for him. In his case it is a life sentence. But what about a younger man? What about his life? He might never see the light of day ever again and probably for a much longer time than the accused in this instance. And all for a crime it is impossible to commit!"

"Lucas, Lucas. It's not so much him I'm concerned about. What will it do to you and your career as a lawyer? Have you thought of that? Don't tell me you actually think you can win with that defence?"

"It's not a question of getting him off scot-free, Ann. I just want to prove that the charge should not be murder since we both know you don't die. So, if you don't die... there is no such thing as murder! What or whom have you killed? You wrecked a 'vehicle', the body. You can certainly kill that. You caused grief and hardship to people. Absolutely, you did all those things. But you *did not murder*! I feel I have to do this, Ann. I can't ask you to work with me as you have in the past. It will have a negative effect on you as well as on me, and I would never do anything to hurt you. You know that. So, I'll leave it up to you. I'll understand however you decide. But I hope you'll stay with me." He reached for her hand and this time it was she who pulled back.

They finished their wine, Lucas paid the bill, and they began their drive back to the city. The only sound heard was the droning of the tires on the wet tarmac. Ann found sensible music on the radio, pushing aside the consternation each was feeling. It was late evening when they arrived at Lucas' home. Ann felt a bit uneasy and wished she was going to her apartment. The SUV was unloaded and they made their way into the house. Still, nothing was said. Finally, Lucas broke the painful silence.

"Ann, I'm sorry about what I told you. Please try to understand my intentions in wanting to do this. I don't want it to come between us. I think the world of you; you must know that." Lucas looked pleadingly at Ann waiting for her to respond. Ann looked at the kitchen floor, tracing circles with one toe. After a time, she looked up at Lucas and held his gaze, finally speaking.

"Lucas, your idea of defending this guilty man, mind you, guilty according to criminal law which has been the benchmark in our democracy for hundreds of years, came out of left field. I tell you I was stunned! It was the most outlandish thing I ever heard. And I could see the excitement and determination in your eyes. Have you looked at your idea objectively? Well, no, you haven't had time yet. But I'm so afraid of the effect it will have on you. You see, Lucas, I have the same feelings for you as you do for me, and I am so conflicted right now." Ann wiped away a tear.

Lucas went to Ann and held her tightly. Ann slowly responded and he could feel her give up.

Lucas whispered in her ear, "I'll make us some coffee."

● ● ● ● ●

Those who see beyond the lies and myths of their culture, will never be accepted by the masses.
- Plato

Lucas and Ann sat at the kitchen table both in an uncomfortable mood. There was still a lot of silence between them. Both were playing out different scenarios in their minds and guesstimating each result and what the effect could be. Lucas spoke first.

"I think the most important part of this whole plan is the opportunity it will present to people to open their minds up to what life and death really mean. Let them see what actually transpires. If they understand just a part of what takes place, enough to make them consider the possibility of never dying, the soul never dying, and that how you live your life really counts for something, well, don't you think that is worthwhile?"

"It's all worthwhile, Lucas, but why you? Is it worth risking everything you've worked your whole life for?" Ann's eyes asked the question too as she placed her hands in pleading supplication. "The worst part is, I'm afraid of what it might do to us." Lucas saw the concern in her eyes.

"But, don't you see? Who I am and what I do is the means of bringing the truth out to the greatest number of people. Being able to use the courtroom as a platform will gain people's interest. Plant the seed, so to speak. I'm no preacher, but I see this whole concept, all that has been shown to us, as the most important undertaking there is. And know this: whatever happens, I will take care of you."

Ann left her chair, sat on Lucas' lap, and put her arms around Lucas' neck.

"I do trust you. You are a good man. And yes, I will stay with you to the bitter end. We'll do this together."

"Thank you, thank you. That means everything to me." He put his arms around her and they stayed like that for a time.

Eventually, Ann climbed the stairs to her bedroom. She felt exhausted from the trip and all that Lucas was proposing. She was apprehensive about what was about to unfold. She feared for Lucas and didn't know why. Eventually sleep overtook her and she dropped off with concerns still swimming around in her subconscious.

Lucas stayed up with his customary bedtime scotch thinking of what he was planning on doing. He was also wondering about Ann and the affection she had shown toward him. It was more than just friendship, Lucas realized. Ann was a terrific friend. Had been for years. But how could he tell her that he had no sexual interest in any woman since Sarah passed. He had thought of it... even with Ann. But, to him, it would have seemed like cheating, even more so after learning about the soul and not dying and hearing messages from Sarah. It was love between he and Ann, but for him it was a platonic love. This was enough for him. He wasn't sure if it would be enough for Ann.

After a light breakfast the following morning they took their coffee to the 'war room' where they firmed plans for the day.

"Our first move must be to see the accused. Evaluate him and learn all we can about him. I want you with me, Ann. And your notepad. He'll be at the lock-up for now. Even though he has confessed, he still has the right to a lawyer. I can't imagine the court will have an easy job finding one. This type of case has no reward of any kind so I won't have to fight a horde of lawyers. I will volunteer my services on his behalf. I'll have to clear it all with the firm. Don't know just how Wiff will take it. I may have to do some fancy dancing with him. Another thing, Ann, a person charged with murder has the right to choose to be tried by judge or jury, and we definitely want a jury trial. Choosing the jury will buy us some time. If all that goes okay, we'll have to line up our witnesses next. Feel up to the day?"

"Oh, yes! We're double harnessed again. Whoopee!"

After making a few phone calls Lucas learned that Joseph Simpson was in a holding cell at the Gottingen Street police station. He and Ann drove to the low brick building and were taken to Simpson's cell. Asking to talk with the accused privately, they were locked in the cell with him.

"Just shout when you want out," the officer told them.

In Joseph Simpson they saw an old man, worn down and hopeless from years living literally from hand to mouth on the city streets. He was grizzled, in desperate need of a shower, a shave, and a haircut. He was far from looking the part of a murderer, but then, Lucas thought, 'What does a murderer look like?'

"Good morning Mr. Simpson. I am a lawyer from the law offices of Brannigan and Clark. My name is Lucas McNab and this is my assistant, Miss Ann Hughes. Do you now have access to a lawyer?"

"No sir, I don't. The police told me since I confessed, I wouldn't need a lawyer."

Lucas gave a disgusted look at Ann and shook his head in disbelief.

"How old are you, Mr. Simpson?"

"I'm seventy-six or thereabouts sir, I guess." Joseph Simpson kept his eyes on the concrete floor.

"How long have you lived on the street here in the city?" Lucas continued.

"Oh, gosh, I don't know for sure. It's been a long time though."

"Do you have family, here or anywhere else in the country?"

"No sir. I don't have any family left. Just me." Simpson shoved his hands in his pockets.

"Mr. Simpson, you do need a lawyer, and I would like to represent you in court. Is that acceptable to you?"

"I guess so, if you say so, Mr. McNab."

"Thank you, Mr. Simpson. Now, you should have a copy of the charge sheet given you by the police. Do you have any papers here with you? That will give the date for your court appearance."

"Nope. They said they would keep papers for me at the desk."

"Mr. Simpson, are you willing to stay here in this cell until we go to court?"

"Oh, yes, Mr. McNab. This is pretty nice. I got a bed, food ain't bad, and it got heat." Joseph smiled and glanced at Lucas.

"Now, Mr. Simpson. I want you to tell me exactly what happened that night you claim you killed... Charles Conlon."

Ann was writing down everything Joseph Simpson was saying.

"Like I told them already. A bunch of us were in the bandstand at the park. I had scored a bottle of Cap'n Morgan so we was passin' it around, tryin' to keep warm. Well, Chucky was gettin' the lion's share and I got mad at him and smothered him with his coat. That's how it happened, sir." Simpson steadily avoided looking ar Lucas.

"You say there were more there than just you and... Chuck in the bandstand. Can you tell me their names?"

"Naw, I didn't really know them other fellers."

"All right, Mr. Simpson. I will stay in touch with you. And don't speak with anyone claiming to be a lawyer. You have your right to remain silent at all times. Do you understand?"

"Yes sir. Don't talk with no one."

"Good. Here's my card, Mr. Simpson. Anyone comes to you, you tell them to contact me, okay? Now we have work to do so we will see you again, soon. Thank you."

Lucas picked up the charge sheet as they left and saw that the arraignment was just two days away at the Provincial Court House, at 10:00 a.m. Stopping at the court house, Lucas informed the clerk that he was representing Mr. Joseph Simpson, being arraigned in two days. After this they stopped in at the Nook where they found one of the two recessed alcoves empty. They ordered espressos and compared notes and thoughts of their meeting with Mr. Simpson.

"So, Lucas. What do you make of Mr. Joseph Simpson?" Ann queried.

"I don't believe he's telling the whole truth of that night. Every street person, every wino, they all know everybody else in their circle. And you don't share a bottle of rum with strangers. Not by a long shot. What do you make of him?"

"I think I agree with you. He didn't show remorse. It was all just matter-of-fact. Of course, what does a person on the street have to lose? He's found a comfortable room that can be his for the rest of his life. Free dental, haircuts, medical, change of sheets, food, hell, it sounds pretty good even to me!" Ann said.

"This is what I was telling you last night. It can do him no harm. I'd be doing him no favour by getting him off and putting him back on the street. Not that I ever could get him off. But we've got to try and find the other guys that were there when the murder took place. I guess my next stop is to tell Brannigan and Clark what's happening.

I don't look forward to that. Ann, are you sure you still want to be a part of my off-the-wall experiment in rewriting criminal law?"

"I do!"

"Well, then. Let's put the wheels of justice in motion. Now, when we get to the firm, you go to my office and stay there. I'll beard the dragons myself. Got that?"

"Got it. Let's go."

At the law firm, Lucas searched out Wiff and Matt. Matt was in court but he found Wiff in his office. Lucas braced himself and went in.

"Ah, there ya are, old son. How ya been? Vacation over, is it?"

"Yes, I started getting bored, Wiff. Had to get back to doing what I do, you know."

Wiff, never taking his eyes off Lucas, said, "Well now, we don't have any cases on the docket at present, Lucas."

Lucas noted that Wiff had dropped his good old boy speech pattern. He had never seen this new mannerism in Wiff before.

"Wiff, I've just come from interviewing the accused in the recent murder and I'd like to mount a defence for him."

"I know all about your visit, Lucas. I have my ways. May I ask what drew you to this particular accused? After all, he confessed, didn't he? And I don't expect there to be any great sum of money to be obtained in this, so I would like to know what in Sam Hill you are up to!"

'Here it comes,' Lucas thought. 'This is where the rubber hits the road, or I do.'

"Matt's in court, I understand. I want him here when I explain my reasons, Wiff."

"That's fair enough, Lucas. Matt should be here too. I believe he's due back around two. It's now ten forty-five. Plan on meeting here 'bout two thirty. How's that?"

"That's good, Wiff. Thanks."

On the drive back to the house, Ann was both anxious and afraid to ask about Lucas' meeting.

"How did the meeting go, Lucas? I'm dying to know."

"Well, it wasn't a meeting. Matt wasn't there so nothing was accomplished. It's been rescheduled for two thirty this afternoon. They're giving themselves time to talk about me, I figure. Wiff knew about us meeting with Simpson. He has contacts all over. He's a sly one. I think we have to be prepared for the worst. I realize they have the reputation of the firm first and foremost to look after and protect. I understand that, but I have interests too that are important to me. We'll just have to wait and see. Are you still okay with everything we talked about?"

"I am. In fact, I'm beginning to see your reasoning a bit clearer now, and I'm fully behind you in whatever you decide."

He reached for her hand, smiled, and nodded his head.

"Something Wiff said bothers me. He made it clear that he has far-reaching contacts that keep him informed on matters that concern him and the firm, matters that are important to the firm I suppose."

She prepared a salad for their lunch and he perked the usual coffee. They sat at the kitchen table and discussed their plans for the upcoming hearing.

"First thing we've got to do is to enter a not guilty plea, which is going to throw the Crown into a fit. They will probably be expecting me to plead down. There'll be an argument there, I'm guessing. But it is just a formality. Everything there will just be a formality, really. We'll ask that the trial be held in the Supreme Court by jury. The other side is not going to be very happy, but they have no choice. We'll pass on the preliminary, and we won't fight them on bail. Simpson's far better off in his cell."

"And what about Mr. Simpson during all of this?"

"Simpson doesn't have to be in attendance but I'll bring him in. I don't believe he'll have much interest in the proceedings. I don't know if making him more presentable is necessary for this show. As for the meeting with Wiff and Matt, I'll do that alone. I would like you to try and get in touch with both Rosalie and Marie, explain fully what we are doing and ask if they would agree to testify for us. Okay?" Lucas asked.

"I can do that. I'll be thinking about you and wishing you luck," Ann answered.

Lucas gave her a big hug and made his way back his vehicle. He was apprehensive about this meeting and had a sense it would not go well for him.

• • • • •

Lucas walked into Wiff's office, went over to where Matt was sitting, and shook his hand. "How did court go, Matt?"

"So-so, Lucas. Wiff here told me some strange plan you have regarding the park murderer. Can you enlighten us?" Matt got right to the point.

Lucas decided to let it all come out. "All right. Here is my reason for defending a murderer. A confessed murderer, but that doesn't matter. I believe... no, I *know* that every person has a soul. This is a fact that can be argued successfully. And another fact is that the soul cannot be destroyed. This too can be argued successfully. Now, our body is just a conveyance, like a car. And like a car it wears out and 'dies' for whatever reason. But the soul *cannot* die. The body can be destroyed by car accident, gunshot, knife, fire, a fall, any number of reasons, but the soul simply leaves the body.

"The soul is taken to another plane, another universe if you will. Therefore, no one can be killed because the soul cannot be destroyed. Hence, no murder has been committed. A murderer, in the traditional sense of the word, hasn't killed anyone. He can be charged with, let's say, arson, or property damage, any number of related felony charges, but not murder. Have I made myself clear?"

There was complete silence. Lucas sat down and looked from one face to the other, waiting for someone to say something. Finally, Wiff Brannigan looked intently at Lucas.

"Have you lost your mind? What in hell are you talking about? I sure don't know. You must be smokin' some bad weed there, old son. Do you actually intend on going forward with that as your defence? You'll be laughed right out of court, you will. Good Lord, man. That is *the* most laughable piece of crap I have ever heard!"

Matt's complexion had paled and he appeared shocked.

"Lucas, I have to admit, I don't follow much of what you said, but I have to agree with Wiff on this. I fear if you follow through with your intention, it might, no, it *will* destroy your future as a lawyer and it certainly will not do much for the firm. The accused means nothing to you. Right now, he is enjoying the best time he's had in, probably years. Let him have his rest. After all, he's only street people. I'm asking, please don't do this. No damage has been done, yet. You've only got a few years until you can retire. Please, don't throw everything away on something that has little or no meaning."

It was pretty much what Lucas had expected. He was positive now that trying to explain further would be useless.

"It has meaning to me, Matt or I wouldn't propose it. If I decide to proceed with my plan, do I have any support from the firm?"

Lucas waited for the answer. Finally, it was Matt who addressed his question.

"Lucas, you are aware, no doubt, that Wiff and I talked about your defending this accused man, before hearing your defence plan. And what you just told us convinces us that you leave us with only one recourse. And I believe you must expect what that will be. I am so very, very sorry, Lucas. But if you go forward with this defence plan of yours ... we will have no choice but to disassociate the firm from you. You will understand why this is what must be done. It will have to be done quickly before any news of this leaks to the media, so we must have your decision by nine o'clock tomorrow morning. It will appear as an amicable parting and you will receive a generous settlement. I expect Ann will stay on here, but on the off chance she decides to assist you, she will be well looked after too. Now, Lucas,

I want you to think hard on this. You and I go back too many years to have it end this way."

Matt walked over and took Lucas' hand in both of his and shook it firmly, looking steadily in his eyes. Lucas truly disliked having to burden Matt this way. Wiff too, for that matter. The meeting brought what Lucas was giving up into sharp focus. He was in no hurry to see Ann.

Lucas had to be alone with his thoughts. He stopped in at the Lion's Head for a scotch and a mind search. It was shocking, although expected, to have his situation laid out so completely, and clearly. He knew it would inevitably turn out like this. Here he was, sixty-nine years old, seventy really, playing fast and loose with his future. And how could he take Ann down with him? She didn't deserve to be put in that sort of a position. Was he acting irrationally after all? Was he just tilting at windmills? Windmills of the mind like the song says? Lots of questions...no answers.

As he opened the front door, Ann was waiting for him. She knew immediately the meeting hadn't gone well. Lucas looked drawn and tired. She hugged him and felt him tremble, just a little. She held him until she felt him relax.

"Come sit down, love. Can I get you another scotch? Anything?" Ann walked him to the living room couch.

"Thanks. Scotch. Please."

She would let him decide when to explain the meeting. She brought him the scotch and a glass of wine for herself and sat close to him.

Lucas laid his head back, eyes closed. He was searching within for the courage to tell her what their options were.

"It was quite the meeting. They weren't crazy about me wanting to defend a confessed murderer, and after I told them *how* I was going to defend him, they thought *I* was crazy! Matthew laid it all on the line. I have until tomorrow morning at nine to decide whether to drop the whole thing or take their severance package. The same offer was made on your behalf."

"Lucas, didn't you, be honest now, didn't you think this is what would happen?"

"You're probably right. Deep down I figured it might be like a windshield wiper on a rooster's behind... it wouldn't work."

The shock was wearing off and he had a clearer head. He took his scotch, placed his arm around Ann's waist, and steered them both to the sunroom.

"Now, tell me how you made out, my girl."

"I had a better day than you did, I would say. I tried contacting Marie St-Onge and had to leave a message. Then I called Rosalie and explained what we were doing. She was a bit reluctant at first but the more we talked, the more interested she became. I think she'll help us out. How's that?"

"Good. That's great! Ann, before we go any further, you have to decide, along with me, what you are going to do. Stay with the firm or work with me. I know you have said you are with me, but you better give it some thought. If you leave the firm, they will give you a good severance package. I think, in the back of their minds, Wiff's in particular, if they don't treat us fairly this scheme might taint the firm somehow and that's working in our favour. So don't say anything now. Sleep on it. We'll decide in the morning. Right? Now, I'm getting another drink. You?"

"I'll get them. Sit still," Ann offered.

Lucas pulled his neck down into his shoulders to ease the tension. He had a bit of a headache and his neck muscles were tight. He concluded he wasn't in the best shape of his life.

Ann returned with a tray containing the drinks along with crackers and cheese.

"Thought you should have something more in your stomach than scotch."

"Thanks. You're right, as usual."

They spent the rest of the afternoon in small talk, not getting into detail about the case. That would start in earnest, or not, after the call tomorrow morning. Ann made a light omelette for their supper and then they went to bed.

• • • • •

If a man does not keep pace with his companions, perhaps it is because he hears a different drummer. Let him step to the music which he hears, no matter how measured or far away.
- H. D. Thoreau

Morning found them up early, neither having slept well. Breakfast consisted of coffee. Lucas posed the question first.

"May I ask what your decision will be?"

Ann looked away and took several minutes to reply. She knew the implications of her decision to stay with Lucas and she trusted him completely. Whatever the future held for her well, that would be it. Besides, it was going to be one hell of a ride, she figured.

"I made my decision days ago, Lucas. I told you I was with you to the end. Nothing has happened to change my mind, and I know what you're going to do."

He wasn't surprised at her answer, but he was relieved.

"Thanks, Ann. I'm not sure what we're getting into, but I'm grateful to have you with me."

The calls to the firm were made and their decisions accepted. Matthew would release the news to the media that Lucas was retiring from the firm to do freelancing and Miss Ann Hughes would be joining him. Lucas and Ann were to clear out their office and pick up their severance packages that day.

Just past nine-thirty they were filling boxes with years of office accumulation. Wiff was nowhere to be seen, but Matt stopped by to wish them both well. The word was out and looks of disbelief were on the faces of staff. Alison showed more remorse than the others.

She and Ann were close friends. She hugged them, dried her tears, and returned to her desk.

They picked up their severance package and made their way to the SUV, each carrying a box of memories.

While driving back to the house, Ann opened their severance and let out a low whistle.

"Lucas! Matt has been very generous to us. Look at these figures."

"Holy! He *was* generous. We'll be good for a while, eh girl?"

They spent the rest of the day in their 'war room'.

"How do you think the trial will play out?"

"Not too sure. The Crown will present their case. Call witnesses from the police on down. I expect they will make light of our address to the jury, make fun of it and make me out to be a fool. We'll suffer abuse, that's for sure. But we stay the course. We'll have good arguments. I think we'll do well. Remember my reasons for attempting this: First, murder can't happen. Second, get people to open their eyes and have them understand their reason for being here. In practical terms the first reason is important to the world, as this concept is earth-shaking. The second reason is on a personal level, not new at all, but important just the same. The accused and the subsequent trial is the vehicle that allows us to reach the public. No harm can be done to Joseph Simpson."

"We've got a lot of work to do. Where do we start?" Ann focused on practical matters.

"Witnesses. We've got to have credible witnesses. Cool under cross examination. Steadfast in their beliefs. Willing to be laughed at in the media and rise above. I don't think we'll need that many. Hopefully I can turn some of the Crown's witnesses to our side. Let's make a list of who we need," said Lucas.

"If Marie St-Onge agrees to work with us, there's our psychic and our medium. And Rosalie, maybe," added Ann.

"We're going to need someone from the clergy who is open-minded to what we're trying to do. That's going to be difficult. Perhaps Marie can help on that. I hope she isn't on a world tour or something," said Lucas.

"What about scientists? Are there any out there who aren't close-minded?" asked Ann.

"Somewhere, probably. Remember Ann, we will cross examine all their witnesses, and their testimony will be questioned. Let's take a break and I'll perk some coffee."

"Doctors?" continued Ann.

"Yes. Doctors, paramedics, firemen, police. Any from those groups might have experienced something regarding the soul," Lucas agreed. " I could really use someone else who was in the bandstand that night. What are the chances of that happening?"

They stood, stretched, and yawned. Lucas brewed coffee while Ann made up a plate of cheese, crackers, and Polish sausage slices.

"You know, I'm getting as excited about our trial as any case I defended with Brannigan and Clark. This one has such an important purpose... to everyone. Do you have that feeling?"

"Yes, I do. It's... it's biblical in some ways. It's hard to describe. I'm happy to be working with you again, Lucas. I understand the importance of what you are doing."

● ● ● ● ●

On the appointed court date, Lucas arrived fifteen minutes early and noted the Crown prosecutor, Michael Sullivan was already there. Michael saw Lucas and gave him a smile and a nod. Lucas returned the nod. His client was brought to the room. Once again, Joseph's appearance left much to be desired. They sat together in the public seats. Since Simpson was represented by a lawyer, his case would be one of the first cases called. In fact, they were the third called. The clerk called Simpson's name and read the charge. Lucas prompted

Joseph to stand and guided him to the front of the court so he was visible to the presiding judge, Arthur Muirhead.

The judge looked at Simpson, then at Lucas, and then he read the charge out loud.

"Joseph Simpson, you have heard the charge against you. Are you prepared to plead?"

Lucas nudged Simpson, who answered in a low voice, "Yes, I am, sir... your Honour."

"Please speak up, Mr. Simpson. How do you plead to this charge?"

"Not guilty."

Lucas could hear the movement of someone leaving the courtroom. He quickly looked around and saw it was Michael Sullivan.

Lucas addressed the judge.

"We wish to dispense with a preliminary hearing and will not be seeking bail, your Honour. We also request trial by jury."

The judge looked long and hard at Lucas.

"Very well, Mr. McNab. Jury selection will begin in fifteen days from this date. If possible, trial will begin one month from this date in the Supreme Court. Leave your contact information with the clerk. Do you have any questions?"

"No, your Honour," said Lucas.

"Guard, take the accused back to his cell," ordered Judge Muirhead.

Lucas quickly asked Joseph if there was anything he needed.

"No, Mr. McNab. I'm good. Thank you."

"I'll see you soon, Joseph."

Lucas left the courthouse feeling like he had just jumped off a cliff. 'Now the work begins,' he thought. He puzzled over the appearance of Michael Sullivan in place of a lesser Crown. It was obvious he was there just to hear their plea. He left in a hurry, taken by surprise, no doubt.

• • • • •

Back home Lucas found that Ann had been cooking. She had a roast in the oven and a pie to follow. The house smelled delightful, and it brought back memories of his Sarah. He found he could reminisce now without having his thoughts gathered in by grief just by knowing she was around him.

"What's going on, girl? What's cooking?"

"I knew we would be going flat out from now on, so I decided to cook something. We don't have to live on pizza and beer. Besides, I haven't had a good reason to cook for a while. I'm enjoying it. How did court go?"

"Court was all right. Joseph was good. We have our dates and we have ample time, I think, to put our case together. Any word from Marie St-Onge?"

"No, nothing yet. There was a strange call by a man who wanted to speak to you. He didn't leave a name and the number was a public phone. Said he'd call back."

Lucas squinted his eyes and tilted his head, trying to place who might have called, then passed it off with a shrug.

"Know who was in court this morning? Michael Sullivan! I think he expected us to plead guilty and plea bargain. When he heard Joseph say 'not guilty', he left like a shot."

"That is strange, isn't it?"

"He must be in a quandary, wondering what our plans are now. We've got to be careful with Sullivan. He has the long arm of the law on his side. What kind of pie did you make?"

• • • • •

Michael Sullivan left the courthouse and was quickly in his BMW, punching in a phone number.

"Hello, Michael. What is it?"

"I just left court and heard McNab enter a 'not guilty' plea! What's going on here?'

"I told ya, old son. Don't take McNab for a fool. I'll give ya his whole defence plan and then I don't wanna see or hear from ya again. Got that?"

"Yes, I've got it."

Having returned to his office he leaned back in his chair and waited for the fax to begin.

• • • • •

Lucas and Ann cleared the big kitchen table for the work ahead of them. He brought out the police information package which only contained the charge sheet, Simpson's confession, and the court date. Everything seemed straightforward. The confession was typed up by the police and signed by Simpson, with two witnesses. He was charged with murder.

"Question: why would Simpson give himself up so quickly and easily? It's as if he was resigned to the consequences of what he had done and was prepared to face them." Lucas answered his own question.

"Maybe he didn't mean to do it. Maybe it was an accident, and he just gave up, feeling remorse," added Ann.

"That could well be. I don't accept his version of what happened, but without a witness, that's all we have to work with. Okay, let's put ourselves in the Crown's boots for now. They know we're going to defend a confessed murderer. They will suspect that we have some extraordinary new evidence for us to go this far. And they have no other course but to base their case on that assumption, that is, until we give them a list of our witnesses, and let's hope and pray we *have* witnesses. Once the cat is out of the bag, they'll have to scramble to find witnesses to counter ours and that shouldn't be easy... unless James Randi, that magician turned debunker, is available. In fact, about all they can do is attempt to disprove what we put forth."

"Who have you in mind for our side?" Ann asked.

"Marie, definitely, if she can. It would do me no good to have to subpoena anyone. They would almost become a hostile witness. What do you think our chances are of finding a clergyman sympathetic to our beliefs?"

"That's a tough one, Lucas. I wouldn't have a clue. Marie might have contacts. She is important to us right now. Where is she?"

"You're right. She's away somewhere and we need her right now. I think we'll have to have someone from the sciences to verify certain aspects of our evidence." Lucas tapped a pencil on the table as he ran names through his mind.

"What about doctors, paramedics, fire rescuers, even police. As we said, they're all involved in life and death situations. Someone must have seen something out of the ordinary, don't you think?"

"Absolutely, Ann. That might be a good place for us to start. Good thinking."

"I'm not just a pretty face... do I have a pretty face?" Ann placed a finger on her cheek and rapidly blinked her eyes provocatively at Lucas

"The prettiest." Lucas gave Ann a big smile.

Just then, Lucas' cell went off.

"Yes?"

"Mr. McNab. I just heard about you defending Joey Simpson. He didn't murder anyone. I know. I was there with him that night. So were others I know."

Lucas motioned for Ann to come close to the phone.

"You're telling me that nobody was murdered that night? The police have a body and Simpson confessed. Explain that."

"No, Mr. McNab, you don't understand. Chucky Conlon was dying of cancer. He'd had it for a while. It got so bad that he begged to be done in. Chucky and Joey were close friends, so Joey decided he'd do it, to help a friend. Joey took what money he had and got a bottle of rum. There were four or five of us and we decided to have a party like, just for Chucky, you see? We made sure Chucky got must of the rum to sorta help him on his way. And when he got pretty drunk, Joey... Joey, he like... smothered him. We all helped him a bit. So you see, Mr. McNab, Joey didn't murder Chucky. He helped him outa his pain."

Lucas couldn't speak.

"Hello, hello... Mr. McNab?"

"What's your name?"

"Frankie. Frankie Malloy, Mr. McNab."

"Frankie, thank you so much for contacting me. I truly appreciate it. How can I reach you?"

"I don't have no address, Mr. McNab, but I hang around the park where Chucky died. That would be the place to look for me."

"Would you be able to testify in court about what you just told me, Frankie?"

"Why, sure, Mr. McNab. You can count on me. Yes sir. Joey's a good man, Mr. McNab."

"Thank you for calling, Frankie." Lucas ended the call, and looked at Ann.

"Assisted suicide. What they allow doctors to do legally. How about that? We knew there was more to the story than what Simpson was telling," Ann said.

"That explains Joseph's demeanor," Lucas said.

"It won't make any difference to the case, though. It could have been pleaded down I suppose, but at Simpson's age it wouldn't make much difference. Anyway, Lucas, that's not what our objective is in this case. We're using the trial as a means to an end."

"I know, I know. But it's good to hear the truth. I have respect for Joseph Simpson for his action. He is a brave, sensitive soul who did the right thing for the right reason. You could say Joseph Simpson is part of our team. He is, in fact. He just won't know it. But Chucky will."

"Well said." Ann smiled. "Want some coffee?"

Shortly after they had lunch, Lucas' phone rang again. This time he recognized the number.

"It's Marie!" he told Ann, before answering the phone. "Hello, Marie. How are you?"

"Fine, Lucas. I just returned from a short vacation in Alberta. What's going on with you these days?"

Lucas told Marie of their plan of trying to eliminate the charge of murder and how it was progressing, and she indicated she was more than willing to help in any way.

"Marie, we've got to get together. There is so much to accomplish and so little time. How long are you home?"

"I have no immediate plans. Besides, this idea of yours absolutely intrigues me. I believe it would take something momentous to interrupt me once we get started."

"We've set up an office here at my house. Is it possible for you to come here?"

"Certainly. When?"

"Whenever you can. We'll be here," said Lucas, pleased with Marie's willingness to help.

Marie St-Onge arrived at the house a few hours after speaking to Lucas.

"Come in, Marie. It's good to see you again. Did you enjoy your trip?" Lucas reached for Marie's coat

"It was good, but I am always glad to return to the East Coast. Hello, Ann, how are you?"

R.B. Brown

"Fine, Marie. Good to have you back."

Lucas and Ann brought Marie fully up to speed on everything. She expressed excitement over the concept of the effect of the soul on murder.

"Marie, we are asking you to be our main witness in this. I know the Crown prosecutor, and if he doesn't bag off, you will be able to tie him up in knots! How about it?" Lucas asked.

"Absolutely. I'd love it," Marie answered.

"That's great! Thank you, Marie. As for the Crown's witnesses, since they believe this to be just another murder trial, they'll have the police boys, Simpson's confession, and maybe the coroner. That's all they would need, normally. But once they see who we're putting on the stand, they won't know what's going on. They won't have much time to round up witnesses either. Then we'll go to work," Lucas explained.

"Lucas, I must tell you, your purpose in this is so important. And you have chosen the perfect stage to present irrefutable proof that we don't die. More and more people worldwide are understanding this. In 2016, the world population was estimated to be 7.4 billion. In 2012 it was estimated that at least six *billion* people are followers of some form of religion that believes in an *afterlife*! You are doing the absolute correct thing." Marie gave Lucas a hug. Ann was watching.

"There is something else we were wondering," Lucas continued. "We should have the clergy on hand, one who understands as we do, along with someone in science who can verify the existence of the soul and can back us up. Would you or could you come up with names? We thought you might have run into this type of person sometime. We don't have a lot of money but we can cover expenses if they're within reason. Could you think about that, Marie?"

"Certainly, Lucas. Anything else I can help with?" Marie responded.

"Just prepare yourself for a bumpy ride!" Lucas smiled.

"Absolutely! I'll get working on this right away. Stay in touch. Bye." With that, Marie waved and let herself out.

Lucas placed his arm around Ann's waist and walked her back to the kitchen.

• • • • •

Michael Sullivan sat in the Chief Crown's office. Sullivan had just informed the Chief Crown about the events surrounding what was supposed to be a simple slam-dunk murder conviction. The Chief Crown, Randal MacDonald, steepled his fingers as he gazed at the harbour from the thirteenth floor window.

"I don't see anything in McNab's intentions to cause us great concern. Actually, the public and the media will laugh him out of court. His case will go nowhere, and neither will he after we're through. His legal career will be finished. Too bad. I always liked McNab. As for witnesses, get a sympathetic clergyman. That shouldn't be difficult. You must have a scientist of some sort to argue the existence of a soul. And, of course, the coroner. Who knows more about dead people than a coroner! And you've got the police, the paramedics, and so forth. Just make sure they're on our side. No matter what McNab might have up his sleeve, just keep in mind this is nothing more than a case of murder. Okay? Now go." The Chief Crown dismissed Sullivan.

Sullivan returned to his office on the same floor. He still had questions. Ever since he had been made aware of Lucas' real intent in bringing the case to trial, and as absurd as McNab's scheme sounded, something bothered him. He had a bad feeling about it. He sensed the Chief was wrong. It was no longer just a 'case of murder'. There was much more to it than that. He went to his computer and started combing through his lists of witnesses.

• • • • •

As Lucas and Ann were absorbed in developing their defence strategy, Lucas' phone went off. It was Marie.

"Hi, it's me, bringing you up-to-date on my activities. I contacted a pastor, whom I've known for years and who understands our beliefs very well. After telling him of your idea, he's all in favour of our efforts and is more than happy to help out. I gave him your number and he'll be in touch. His name is Harris.That's one big problem solved. I'm still working on the second part."

"That's wonderful news, Marie. I've asked the Crown for their list of witnesses but I don't have it yet. I expect it will just be the usual list since they are not aware of our plans. We've been working out our strategy. I'll have to go to jury selection soon, I suspect. That might take a couple of days. We'll be in good shape. As I told you, you are our most important witness, so don't neglect preparing yourself. After I talk with the pastor, we'll get together and do you... sorry, well, you know what I mean. Take care, Marie, and good luck."

"Cheers, Lucas." Marie ended the call.

"There, we have the religious aspect of our case hopefully taken care of. You were right in assuming Marie would know all sorts of people in all fields." Lucas softly pinched Ann's cheek.

"You are so smart! What's next?" asked Ann.

"Let's grab a bite to eat. You know, we've got to do something about Simpson's appearance for court. We mustn't forget that." Ann started for the kitchen

"Absolutely. He's being held at the correctional facility in Dartmouth now, eh?"

"Oh, that's right. I forgot about that. I don't think it makes any difference to him. He's better off than he's been for years. Here he is, the centre of what will be, without doubt, the biggest trial in the history of Canadian law! And he's completely oblivious to it all."

Lucas stared at Ann in concern. He hadn't thought of what they were attempting in that frame of reference and he quickly evaluated the risk involved in his plans. Lord, there wouldn't be enough lawyers in the land to handle the re-trials and law suits!

"Are you okay, Lucas?" Ann asked, with some concern.

Lucas was still looking at Ann with a blank stare. He shook his head and blinked.

"What?... Yeah, I'm good. You caught me by surprise when you said 'the biggest trial in the history of Canadian law'."

"Well? Won't it be? Perhaps it will change laws all over the world!"

"Stop it, Ann. You're making me quite nervous now." Some of the colour had left Lucas' face.

"I'm sorry, Lucas, but surely you had considered the impact this would have, even if we lose the case. The repercussion will be felt worldwide."

Ann wasn't helping Lucas adjust his thinking. Was he doing the right thing? He walked to the window over the kitchen sink, leaned on the counter, and carefully went over in his mind all the reasons he had for embarking on this journey. He and Ann had already paid a price and he knew there would be more dues to pay. Lucas felt Ann softly rubbing his back and it broke his train of thought. He lowered his head, turned, raised her face gently, and gave her a kiss. His arms gathered her in a close embrace. At that moment they were two against the world.

• • • • •

Michael Sullivan had finally located his kind of preacher: Reverend George Mumford of the Church of Everlasting Light in Lower Sackville. He didn't have to coax very hard, as the good Reverend was elated to have such a platform to espouse his beliefs. Michael had explained what was required and all the Reverend asked for was a time and place. One down, one to go. Michael scrolled through the records in search of the correct kind of scientist he could use to argue the existence of a soul in man. This search was more difficult, but a name eventually came to light - a physicist from Cape Breton. He was both old and old school, the perfect combination, Michael thought. He asked his secretary to contact Sidney Overstreet and give him an outline of their requirements with the usual compensation. There would be no problem with Dr. Farmer, the coroner. Other than lining up what police were involved, all bases were covered. Michael felt somewhat better about the trial.

He went out to get some 'not-so-fresh' air and a coffee, and began to wonder just what exactly was driving Lucas McNab in his mad dash to destruction. He has to have a serious belief in something to carry it to this extreme. 'He appears confident, all right. It will be interesting to learn just who his witnesses are,' Michael mused. He considered doing some research for himself but decided to depend on his witnesses being able to thwart all positions by McNab.

Michael began to evaluate his choice of witnesses. Let's see, his clergyman, Reverend Mumford. 'Old school. Able to preach fire and brimstone, which a lot of people still appreciate,' Michael thought. That should work fine. And again, old Sidney should be able to hold what little knowledge the jury might have regarding science to basic, simple, understandable research and outcomes. Michael felt comfortable in thinking he would be able to make Lucas McNab the laughing stock of 'lawyerdom'.

He next considered the jury. Strange, Lucas never made one challenge. Not one. Surely he must have had concerns over at least one juror. Michael thought that very odd. It was as if McNab didn't care. The jury would be made up of seven men and five women. They included a banker, an auto mechanic, a high school teacher, a mother, an unemployed bus driver, a hairdresser, a waitress, a grandfather, a young lady musician, a nurse, a clergyman (Michael thought for sure Lucas would have challenged him), and finally, an unemployed father of three. About as diverse a jury as you could find. They had picked the banker, Edward Thompson, as their foreman. That motley crew would decide on the success or failure of his part of the trial. Michael Sullivan gave a mental shrug of his shoulders and walked to his car.

• • • • •

"Hi, it's Marie. I'm calling to tell you I think I've located the scientist we need. I told him of your intentions and he is completely thrilled and excited to be part of it. He is extremely knowledgeable regarding the ongoing physics research. He's in the US and will travel at his own expense, dear soul," Marie informed Lucas.

"That doesn't seem right, Marie. Tell him we'll cover expenses while here," Lucas offered.

"Actually, Lucas, he'll probably stay with me. We know each other quite well and we'll have a lot to discuss. I don't believe we require more witnesses in that line, do you?"

"I trust your decision on that, Marie. When is, what's his name, arriving?"

"My apologies Lucas. His name is Andrew Cushing, Dr. Andrew Cushing, and he's retired from JM Aeronautical in Florida. He should he here in a couple of days. I'll pick him up at the airport. If you are home we'll drop by, if that's all right."

"Absolutely. Thanks Marie. See you then."

Lucas sat down at the kitchen table which was covered in paper. He and Ann had been writing down plausible questions that could be used by the Crown against their witnesses.

"Marie came through again, bless her soul."

"Yes. Bless her." Ann rolled her eyes.

"I've been thinking about having Rosalie as a possible witness. What do you think? Granted, she's another medium, but she's a different cut than Marie. I'd like to have her on call."

"You're right; she has a different approach than Marie. Not as polished and that might resonate with a jury. She's down-to-earth and she's just a lovely lady. Sullivan wouldn't be able to attack her very easily. I'll ask her. We thought of her earlier. Transportation to and from Prospect is the only thing, I'm quite sure she doesn't drive," Ann noted.

"We can work something out. I'll call right now." Lucas reached for his phone. "Hello, Rosalie. This is Lucas McNab. Remember me?"

"Oh, hello Mr. McNab. Certainly I remember you. What can I do for you?"

Lucas explained very carefully what they were planning and why they would like to have her as a witness. There were long pauses, but Rosalie did agree to take part.

"Thank you so much, Rosalie. I'll be in touch very shortly," Lucas said gratefully.

"Hey there, Tonto... break time for the band, is it not?" Lucas slapped out a drum roll on his thighs.

"You betchum! You water the horses and I'll get the beans on."

Ann made up roast beef sandwiches with a small leftover salad. Sheets of paper were pushed aside and they sat together, ate, and talked.

Later on, they decided to watch the news of the day and take a breather. Sitting on the sofa together, half listening and half watching the TV, a news item caught Ann by surprise.

"Lucas! Listen!"

Lucas opened his eyes and strained to hear whatever it was Ann was referring to.

"... and we have learned from a reliable source the lawyer representing Joseph Simpson, the accused murderer of Charles Conlon, will be using, as his defence, his claim that there is no such thing as murder. He will be presenting witnesses in an attempt to show that the soul of a person lives on after death and that no one truly dies. We will be following the trial closely and will keep you up-to-date..."

Lucas, now wide awake, was standing and staring at the screen. He couldn't believe what he had just heard. He turned to Ann. His face had lost all colour.

"I don't believe it! Someone contacted the media! Damn, damn, damn. This is not good. The judge will be calling any time now. How will this affect our defence? Jeez, Ann! What's going on?"

His phone sounded. 'That's the judge,' he thought.

"This is McNab," Lucas answered.

"Oh, Lucas! I just heard on the TV. How could this happen? Who's behind it, do you think?" It was Marie.

"I have no idea, Marie. It puts pressure on Judge Muirhead, as well as the rest of us. The Judge will want to see us as soon as possible, I expect. Hang in there and I'll stay in touch. Thanks for calling." Lucas said goodbye to Marie and ended the call.

"If Sullivan doesn't call it won't look good for him," Ann commented.

"That's the way I'd take it, too, Ann."

Lucas reacted quickly to his phone ringing once again. "Hello."

"Lucas, did you catch the news just now?" It was Michael Sullivan.

"I sure did, Michael. What do you make of it? To me, it appears someone is trying to undermine our trial. Any ideas?"

"None, Lucas. No doubt your first choice would have been my office, but I assure you, nothing would be gained by me in doing something like this. It wasn't me. If Judge Muirhead knows about it we'll be getting a call very soon."

"The judge must be yelling bloody murder, if he knows. Thanks for calling, Michael. I appreciate it. If the informant doesn't involve any of us or the judge, who does that leave?" Lucas asked.

"We'll probably never find out. I'll bet even the judge won't be able to obtain answers. Well, Lucas, I'll see you with the judge. Mind your back and be careful," Michael advised.

"You too, Michael."

● ● ● ● ●

When you tear out a man's tongue, you are not proving him a liar.
You're only telling the world that you fear what he might say.
- George A. A. Martin - A Clash of Kings

It was near midnight when Lucas arrived at Judge Muirhead's residence. Seeing the silver Mercedes Lucas knew that Michael was already there. He had barely knocked when the door opened and there stood the judge. Neither spoke as Michael followed the judge to his study. Michael stood by a floor-to-ceiling bookcase, looking pale and very concerned. He and the judge had been having a heated discussion, Lucas surmised. Lucas was shown a chair which he took, immediately wishing he was back home with Ann. The judge sat behind his large desk looking sterner than either of the two men could remember.

"Now then, gentlemen, who can tell me what just happened to my trial? I want answers. I told you we were on thin ice and tonight the ice is developing cracks. Well?" demanded the judge.

Michael went first. "Judge, there was no information leaked from my office, as I told you. There was only the Chief Crown and myself who knew Lucas' plan. I will admit, I think his defense is completely idiotic and am looking forward to being able to show him just that. But I wouldn't stoop to something this low. I have no idea who is behind this, this... crap!"

The judge nodded his head as he studied the calendar pad on his desk. Then, under bushy eyebrows, he looked sternly at Lucas.

Lucas spoke. "Judge, I would only be hurting myself if you thought I had anything to do with this. Lord, I don't know how much damage has been done to my case. Look, nobody in this room had anything to gain by leaking information on my defence of Mr. Simpson. So, it came from someone outside. Michael, I am very concerned to learn that you know about our defence plan."

The judge also was interested in that fact but this leak was more important right now. He had simmered down somewhat, enough to offer a drink to the two lawyers, which they readily accepted. The study was as quiet as a library, each man lost in his own thoughts. Lucas suddenly looked over at Michael.

"Wait just a damn minute. Michael, you just said the only ones who knew of my defence plan were you... and the Chief Crown, didn't you? You didn't know anything about it until, I'm guessing, the Chief told you. Am I correct?"

Michael nodded his head in agreement. The judge looked intently at Lucas.

"Then the big question is... how did the Chief learn about it? I think I know." Lucas felt the judge's eyes on him.

Lucas looked off through the darkened window of the study. The source of the leak hit him in the chest. He would have to let the judge know.

"It's obvious to me. The leak had to come from... Wiff Brannigan."

Judge Muirhead straighten up in his chair.

"Wilfred Brannigan? Brannigan and Clark? That is a serious allegation, Lucas. On what do you base your accusation?"

Lucas would have to disclose more than he wanted to, but it had to be done.

R.B. Brown

"Judge, when I was still a member of that law firm, I approached both Wiff and Matt Clark with my idea to defend Mr. Simpson, including the basis of my defence. I didn't retire from the firm or decide to strike out on my own. Instead, I was given the choice of dropping my plan to defend Simpson or leave the firm. Now, I know both Wiff and Matt very well. And I assure you, Matthew Clark would never stoop to something as low as this. But Wiff? Absolutely, Judge. Absolutely. He has contacts at all levels throughout the city and beyond, He knew about my visit to the jail to see Simpson within hours after I left," Lucas said firmly.

"I admire your honesty in this. True as this may be, I'm afraid nothing can be done to correct it. The cat is out of the bag and you'll never get it back in. You're going to proceed, I expect," the judge said. Turning to Michael, he asked, "What about you, Michael? This hasn't really had any effect on your case, has it?" asked Judge Muirhead.

Michael had been awfully quiet through all of this, just listening and drinking. He could feel rivulets of sweat running down his back as Lucas came closer and closer to the truth. He wasn't completely out of the woods but he could see a small clearing ahead. He had already decided that the Chief didn't need to know any of this.

"You all right, Michael?" the judge asked.

Looking at Michael Lucas saw a colourless face and blinking eyes, beads of perspiration stood out on his forehead.

"Yes. I'm... I'm good," stammered Michael.

"Gentlemen, you're no doubt aware of my feelings when I was first presented with Lucas' defence plan. I was infuriated. I was disgusted. But deep inside I saw the fire in this... elderly lawyer, and I said, good for him. I thought this could well be his last hurrah, and mine too if I go along with it, and I said to myself... let's do it! I believe I'm more committed to it now. The price already paid by Lucas proves to me that he totally believes in what he is doing, that there's something here that has to be brought to people's attention. Mind you, in my courtroom I will be the unbiased judge. I will be fair to both sides. And let me be clear: everything discussed here tonight will stay here.

Understood, Michael? Lucas?" Both lawyers acknowledged the Judge."
Fine. And now, gentlemen, here's to the trial!"

"To the trial!" The last time the three would be in unison.

The two adversarial lawyers left Judge Muirhead's house together.
When they reached their vehicles Michael turned to Lucas, proffered
his hand, and wished Lucas 'good luck'. Lucas returned the wishes,
feeling a bit unsure of Michael's sincerity. Something was not sitting
well with him regarding the Crown Attorney. He would find answers
eventually but now he just wanted to get home to Ann.

• • • • •

It was close to one o'clock when Lucas pulled into his 'parkway'.
He expected Ann to be asleep but she opened the door for him and
hugged him. She didn't speak. She tried to read the outcome of the
meeting in his eyes, and she couldn't.

Lucas put his arm around Ann's shoulder as they walked down the
hall to their war room. Ann took his coat as he settled into the leather
chair. She put his coat away, made a scotch for him, and grabbed the
bottle of wine. She saw his head laid back and his eyes were closed.

She held the glass out to him. "Want to talk?"

"Thanks. Actually, the meeting went quite well. When I first saw
the judge I almost peed myself, I was so nervous I was close to creating
another leak! Michael was already there. I eventually came to the
conclusion that the leak had to have come from Wiff Brannigan..."

"You really think he would do something like that?"

"Who else could it be? I'd be shooting myself in the foot if I'd done
it. Michael is so sure of success he wouldn't have to do it. And the
judge? Has there been any more on the news?" Lucas asked.

"It's been strangely quiet. They'll be digging behind the scenes,
you can bet. Wait until the trial starts... oh, boy! Marie called again

and we had a talk. The leak has bolstered her resolve. She is feisty, let me tell you!" Ann said.

"Okay. Tomorrow we get serious with our witnesses. I don't think we can safely use this house for preparation. The news hawks will be watching it. So, how about your place? They don't know about the apartment, not yet." Lucas looked to Ann for conformation.

" My apartment is small as you know, Lucas, but we can squeeze everybody in."

We'll begin with the minister. Call Marie in the morning and get his number. I can't wait on him to call me. We can prep Marie last, if she even requires prepping. I'm not quite sure how I'm going to use Rosalie. I'll play it by ear."

Lucas started the morning by driving slowly around the Public Gardens, looking for Frankie Malloy. 'Cripes,' he thought, 'I don't even know what he looks like.' He drove down Spring Garden Road, past the main gate, and didn't see one street person. He turned left on to South Park and again, the street was bare of humanity. Another left turn put him on Sackville Street, also bereft of life. Where was everyone? He parked and walked through the corner gate into the Gardens. He managed to find a security guard and asked him about the street people.

"I'm afraid you're too early. They don't get here until late afternoon, or even after dark."

He would have to come back later. He needed Frankie to testify to what really happened that night Charles Conlon lost his life. Joseph deserved to have the truth known about his motive.

Lucas walked to the compact, ornate little bandstand. It was wonderfully constructed, dating back to 1887. Actually, the Public Gardens were a tribute to former city fathers, when you considered the area was once just a swamp covered with brambles. And now, look at it. One of the finest surviving examples of a Victorian garden in North America. Not a bad place to free the soul.

Lucas wondered how Ann was making out. She had planned to try and get someone from the ambulance service and the various fire departments to testify about any out of the ordinary experiences encountered on any of their calls. He decided to give her a call.

"Hi, Lucas. Where are you?" Ann asked.

"I'm cruising down Summer Street hoping to find some summer. How about you?"

"I'm not having much luck. I'll tell you about it later. Did you find Frankie?" Ann was hopeful.

"No. I'm not having any better luck than you are. Let's get a coffee. Where are you?" asked Lucas.

"I'm close to the MacDonald Bridge," Ann replied.

"Okay. There's a Timmy's on Duke. Meet you there."

Ann brought Lucas up to date. "I ran into troubling responses this morning. I think we're being frozen out by someone. No one from either department had anything to say. It was as if they had been cautioned about speaking to us. It was weird."

"That wouldn't surprise me any. In fact, nothing related to this case would surprise me anymore. I'll have to go back to the Gardens tonight to try and locate Frankie. And if I find out someone has talked to him..."

"Well then, what do we do now?" Ann asked, looking puzzled.

"Not much until our witnesses get here. And we don't panic. Keep in mind all we have to prove is... we don't die!" Lucas laughed and grabbed for Ann's hand.

"I suppose we could prepare Marie and Rosalie," Ann suggested.

"That's right. Check with Marie. See if she's home and if she's up for a visit."

Marie was home and anxious to meet with them.

Ann left her Jeep in paid parking and climbed in the SUV with Lucas. Crossing the bridge, Lucas noticed a large, black SUV behind them. He checked a couple of times but didn't think too much of it. The vehicle followed them up Portland Street, maintaining the same distance. The continued presence of the SUV was beginning to concern Lucas a bit, so instead of turning in to the apartments, he began a maze drive through the Dartmouth streets to Cherry Brook, then looped back to Portland. The black vehicle was still behind them and made no effort to disguise its purpose.

"We're being followed. I don't want to expose Marie, and so we won't stop at her place. I'll try and lose him back in the city. What in hell is going on here? Better give Marie a call and tell her about this. Tell her to be careful too," Lucas instructed Ann.

Arriving at Ann's parking lot, the following vehicle slowed down but did not stop. They waited to see if it doubled back but they saw no sign of it. They drove back to the house without incident.

Over coffee at the kitchen they looked at each other.

"What was that all about?" Ann showed some concern.

"I would say somebody is trying to put a scare in us. Somebody knows what we're doing and they don't like it. That's what it seems like to me. That's probably as far as it goes. We'll be alright," assured Lucas.

"Shouldn't we report it to the police?" asked Ann.

"What did you tell me earlier, about the tight-lipped responses you were getting? Besides, it's only a perception on our part. Nothing they could act on. We'll be okay."

By late afternoon Lucas had received a call from Marie's clergy contact, one Simon Harris in Georgia. He told Lucas he was extremely interested in what he was undertaking. He would need a week to settle things where he was teaching and gave a date on which to expect his arrival in Halifax. Lucas filled him in on the basics to date and said he was anxious to meet him.

• • • • •

While they waited for Marie's 'recruits' to arrive with her, they tied up loose ends. Lucas eventually found Frankie Malloy and set up a means of staying in contact with each other, Frankie using a public phone. Lucas gave him some money and threatened him to use it only on clothes, which he did, at the Sally Ann, leaving him money for wine.

Finally, the day arrived when Marie called to say Andrew Cushing had arrived and Reverend Harris was due to arrive on the following day. That left three days to the trial, making their preparation time tight. Marie added that Reverend Harris was bringing his wife and teenage daughter, as the family was planning to have a holiday after the trial. They were booked in at the Westin on Hollis Street. Lucas asked Ann to make arrangements with the hotel to cover the cost of their rooms. Marie intended to put Andrew up at her apartment.

To Lucas it looked like all the bases were covered.

"We should welcome the Harris family, perhaps take them out to dinner?"Lucas suggested.

"Yes. We should. How would it be if we waited until Cushing gets in tomorrow, and then take everyone out?"

"That makes more sense. It gives the Harris' time to settle in. I'll give them a call tonight. How are we doing, Ann? Are we missing anything?" asked Lucas.

"I don't think so. We'll know better once we meet our witnesses and find out more about them. I think they'll do fine. Thanks to Marie, we are fortunate to have them."

"We're *more* fortunate to have Marie! What say I make reservations at McKelvie's for tomorrow night, say, for seven?" Lucas asked enthusiastically.

"That would be wise. Make it seven for seven." She put on a big 'happy face' for Lucas.

Later that night after Ann had turned in, Lucas went to the 'war room'. They hadn't spent much time there lately; their 'army' was growing too big. He sat down and looked at his Sarah's picture. He studied it as thoughts ran through his mind. And then he spoke to her.

"Lord, Sarah, what am I getting into? I need to talk to you. You could always bring me to heel when I got 'crazy' with ideas like this. You were the calm one and I depended on you. I'm asking for guidance from you and anyone else there to help us get this message out to the people. I'm going to be busy for the next while but I promise to contact you when this is all over. I miss you, hon, and I love you. Watch over us. Suddenly, there was a distinctive ;click' and Lucas turned quickly in the direction of the sound. He managed to catch a glimpse of a dime rolling off the edge of the glass-topped table and falling to the floor. He picked it up having no idea where it came from at first. Then he turned to Sarah's picture, smiled and acknowledged the sign she had just given him. He was alright then.

• • • • •

The next afternoon Marie brought Andrew Cushing to Ann's apartment. Lucas was pleased to finally meet this man Marie had spoken of. He was slightly younger than Lucas and looked as if he took care of himself. They involved themselves in small talk while Ann made refreshments. Lucas quickly brought the trial to focus.

"Andrew... may I call you Andrew? I expect Marie has briefed you already on the general parameters of the trial and what will be required from you. Marie indicated that you are a 'new thinker', as they call us, and therefore should have no trouble with the prosecutor and his cross. You will also know my motives in bringing a confessed murderer to a jury trial. We have thought this through and are willing to accept consequences, of which there could be many. What questions do you have?"

Andrew Cushing set his glass on the table and studied Lucas' face.

"Lucas, when Marie first contacted me and told me your intentions, I was floored! My first reaction was... what a brilliant idea! My second thought was what an awful price he's going to pay. Then, the more I dissected the plan the more I became convinced it could work. You do realize, don't you, that there will be, or already are, unknown forces forming up against you? I mean, you are really shaking the tree on this, and you must be careful of what falls out."

"I hear you, Andrew. Three days ago, we were followed, quite openly, by a big, black SUV. I mean, somebody was delivering a message, that was plain," Lucas said.

"That's what I'm talking about. I come from a once proud nation that now looks worse than the Western frontier of 1880. We are controlled twenty-four seven. Well, you get the news, Lucas. You're aware of the shootings. My Lord, to date there have been over eighty persons found dead who were all connected to alternative health care. And it's just accepted by the people," Andrew said sadly.

"I can see an awakening in the young people, Andrew. Some are facing the cold hard truth that higher learning and the attending costs will not always guarantee success. They're finally realizing that working with your hands, the trades in other words, will be where their future lies. Cripes, I've been trying to get some outside panting done for two years! You have to book ahead for trades people these days."

"Let's get to your trial. I think I can handle the prosecution. Science has been opening their eyes and people are now paying serious attention to the paranormal. Some are even admitting to the existence of the soul. The close-mindedness of the past is diminishing. I've got a lot of ammunition, please excuse the term, so I wouldn't be concerned, Lucas," said Andrew.

"Thank you for agreeing to help us on this, Andrew, and a pleasure to meet you. Will you be staying with Marie then?" Lucas queried.

"I believe so. She graciously offered me her guest room. It will be an opportunity to catch up on each other. Oh, and Lucas, I was sorry to learn of your loss. I have been there and know what you've gone through," Andrew said kindly.

"Thank you, Andrew. We've made reservations for supper tonight at McKelvie's. Seven o'clock. Hope that's okay," said Lucas.

"Perfect. See you at seven then."

Marie gave Lucas a brief hug goodbye and they left.

That evening Lucas and Ann picked up the Harris family at the Westin - Simon; his wife, Virginia; and their fifteen-year-old daughter, Rebecca. He had a good feeling about this man too. They arrived at the restaurant and were taken to one of the raised areas off the main floor. Lucas had decided it would afford them some privacy. Marie and Andrew arrived shortly after.

Marie and Ann provided information and suggestions on the various entrées. Lucas answered questions about the city, the province, the political situation, higher education facilities, and the background of the trial. He too asked questions about family backgrounds, what brought them to their beliefs, and the political situation in the States. Lucas quickly realized that the Harris' just might be considering a move to the province, especially when they heard about the number of universities. Simon Harris was not a young man, Lucas guessed. Age showed on his face and carriage, a result of espousing his beliefs no doubt. His wife, Virginia, was a pleasant, upbeat person. Lucas knew the type. Strong-willed and supportive. The type of partner that made it possible for husbands like hers to stand tall amidst the accusations and rhetoric they both surely endured. Then there was Rebecca. Ann made sure she was not neglected. She was polite and well-mannered but Ann noted an uneasiness about her. She too had suffered, at the hands of classmates programmed by closed-minded parents. Tonight she showed enjoyment in her chance to experience new surroundings.

All in all, it was a very pleasant evening. Everyone seemed comfortable with each other. Lucas set a time for the men and Marie to meet the following morning at Lucas' house as it seemed the press were waiting for the trial to start and were, at present, behaving quite sensibly. Virginia and Rebecca would explore the city.

• • • • •

Lucas and Ann managed to have breakfast and make up sandwiches for lunch before Marie arrived with Simon and Andrew. Ann took them into the living room where everyone would be comfortable. Lucas offered coffee and all accepted but Simon, who explained he was undergoing withdrawal from caffeine. Ann mentioned Rosalie as being part of their defence but wasn't sure she would make it today. Lucas explained her importance and how she had been instrumental in giving him the inspiration for what he was undertaking.

Andrew Cushing was the first to speak.

"Tell me, Lucas. What in the world caused you to come to this conclusion, which, by the way, I think is brilliant? As a scientist I am most interested in the outcome of the trial. You are absolutely bang on in your thinking. I am astounded that no one has considered this before!"

Lucas replied, "It was a combination of different factors. The basic idea just came to me. I had it in my mind for a while before I put it before Ann. She's always been my sounding board when we worked together. She thought I was nuts and she nearly convinced me that I was! Then this murder took place and as I learned of the characters involved, well, it presented a perfect scenario for me to do this, right now. I'll admit it appears to have taken a turn I should have anticipated but didn't."

Simon Harris spoke to Lucas' last comment.

"Lucas, you must be aware at all times. You must understand the full ramifications of what you are doing, regardless of the outcome of the trial. I have no idea how many levels of government, in how many countries, how many religions, how many businesses concerned with death, would be affected by you winning this trial. The list is endless. The question is, how far would some of these affected concerns go to protect the status quo? I have come to believe people's souls are, no, *have been* programmed by the social media, our educational systems, contrived protests, the mainstream media, I'm speaking of my country now. The people have no idea of the freedoms lost, and they keep asking for *more* laws! For the most part, they have no self awareness. They are losing their souls. They're turning their souls over to evil willingly!" Simon's passion was evident. "...and herein endeth the lesson. I apologize for preaching at you, Lucas."

"Simon is right, Lucas," added Andrew.

"But here's the thing. All I need is a hung jury to prove my point. One out of twelve. I'm wanting to open people's minds to accept the existence of the soul and how it will change our world and make it a saner place to live. I know it is a risky undertaking but I know my soul will take care of me... and Ann's will take care of her," Lucas added with certainty.

Marie had been quiet while the discussion took place, taking in every word. "Do you not think the people are starting to open up their minds to this type of new idea? The young people, anyway? I find more and more young adults from all walks are becoming interested in alternatives to what they have lived with all their lives. And they are serious. You are correct, Simon, when you point out who will be most unsettled and afraid of what Lucas is proposing. Something else enters into the equation: there are people already knowledgeable about life after death who will be supportive of Lucas. He won't be alone. Remember that, Lucas. Every psychic, every medium, every practitioner of every phase of the paranormal will be lining up to support you."

"Thanks, Marie," Lucas said. "We just might need them all before this settles down. I want you to remember this one thing: the whole purpose of this trial is to present solid evidence to the fact that we all have souls, and the soul has a bearing on how we live our lives, and just as important, perhaps more importantly… we don't die. I simply want people to hear what you have to say and I want them to think. To open their minds. I would like to take away their fear of dying. It was never my intention to try and absolve Joseph Simpson of the charge of murder; he simply provided a perfect opportunity. I have questioned how everything fell so neatly into place and who or what is responsible. Joseph Simpson will end up as a footnote, but a warm and comfortable footnote."

"Well said, Lucas," said Simon. "I recently read a quote that stated, 'seeing the grave as the end of life is like seeing the horizon as the end of the ocean'. Rather well-put, don't you think? Here is what I perceive to be the problem regarding orthodox religion, and it has been for thousands of years: by believing in God alone, it follows that God also is blamed for everything. Therefore there is no release for the people. No purpose. Doesn't it stand to reason that if you believe there is nothing beyond the grave, life loses meaning? You just 'are'?"

"I like that, Simon. That quote could be our slogan. Print t-shirts and everything," said Marie, smiling.

"So! We have one day before the trial. How do you all feel about testifying? Confident enough? I don't believe the prosecution has the ability to carry their case against our arguments, but, as usual, it will be up to the jury. Address your answers directly to the jury. Make them part of the process; don't treat them as invited bystanders. I will present the topic in general terms and let you expand upon it. Does that sound okay to everyone?" The group all expressed their satisfaction with Lucas' points.

" Excellent. I don't believe the Crown will have enough knowledge on our topics to even cross-examine any of you. What say we have a bite to eat," Lucas finished.

The chatter over lunch was light and cordial. It was apparent to Lucas that all three felt confident in their beliefs and ability to perform on the witness stand.

There was a light tapping on the front door and when Ann opened it there stood Rosalie Francoer, her face beaming as usual. Ann reached over and hugged her.

"Rosalie, oh it's so good that you made it! Come in and meet the rest of the team. How did you get here?" Ann asked.

"A cousin of mine drove me in. When I told him what was going on he got so excited. I'm a celebrity in Prospect now, you know!" Rosalie laughed. " He's gone back to Prospect."

"Rosalie, this is Marie St. Onge, a medium like yourself; the Reverend Simon Harris; and Andrew Cushing. Andrew is our science department."

Rosalie shook hands with all three and took the chair next to Simon.

"Can I get you something to eat, Rosalie?" Ann asked.

"We had a little something on the drive up here, but a cup of tea would be nice."

"Certainly. Coming right up!"

Simon turned to Rosalie and brought her into the circle of strangers, making her part of the group.

"Tell me, Rosalie, how did you come to have your psychic ability?"

Rosalie gave him a condensed version. Simon was intrigued with the encounter at the post office and studied Rosalie as she talked. Marie and Andrew were also listening intently.

"And you've seen the afterlife, I understand. Can you describe what it is like? What you saw there?" Simon wanted to learn as much as he could from this unassuming little lady, and Rosalie graciously complied.

After Rosalie had shared her story, Lucas suggested everyone stretch their legs and have a walk about. It was a pleasant day for a change and they toured the back deck and yard. There were a few birdsongs heard, though not many, and Andrew commented on the fact. Rosalie enjoyed not having to fight the wind that always seemed to blow at Prospect. They talked amongst themselves, like old friends already. There was an uncommon silver cord tying them all together.

It was early afternoon when Lucas called them back into the living room. Any questions, loose ends, and concerns had to be addressed. He cleared his throat and began:

"The prosecutor has requested that all witnesses be kept out of court so their testimony will not be contaminated, so to speak, from listening to other testimony. I have no idea if we'll be given time to present anything from our side or not on the first day. Simon and Andrew, I think you should be available for the afternoon session, just in case. After I hear their witnesses I'll have a better idea on what you two will need to cover. Rosalie, you and Marie can have tomorrow off, and I've set up the den for you to stay over if you want. I think you should. You don't have to make that drive twice a day. I expect that you and Marie will have lots to talk about. You just make yourself at home. You too, Marie. Ann will pick you up at around one o'clock, Simon. Bring something to read and some water! You too, Andrew, and if Marie brings you here we can all go to court in my car. Is that okay with everyone? I think I've covered everything. Any questions? If not, let's have a coffee, or tea."

Simon was the first to speak. "When the British surrendered at Yorktown in 1781, their band marched them out to the tune *The World Turned Upside Down*! I've got to find the music to that again. It's more appropriate now."

"Ain't that the truth. I came across an interesting bit of news while researching. I've got it here somewhere." Lucas shuffled papers." Here it is. It was broadcast on the CBC News on January 29 of this year. Listen: 'Smiths Falls company that dissolves the dead has license suspended.' How about that? This is a new 'recycling' technology called 'bio-cremation'. The CBC says dead bodies, well I hope they're dead, I wouldn't want to see 'live' bodies used! The dead bodies are liquefied with a process that blends water with an alkali solution, under pressure. Nothing is said about the toxic and heavy metals in all our bodies and what happens to those. The end product is drained into the sewer system and, listen to this: cities all across this continent collect this 'biosludge' as it is called, and it ends up being dumped on *food crops!* Shades of *Soylent Green.* Remember that movie? And listen to this: the Bereavement Authority of Ontario suspended their license because they didn't have a 'Class One funeral director present'. I had no idea that the funeral directors had a lobby. It appears to be just one step removed from cannibalism to me. What say you, Andrew?"

"Wow! And this is where, exactly, Lucas?" asked Andrew.

"Smiths Falls, Ontario is where the bodies are 'recycled', but the sludge on food supplies has been going on for a time, I suspect in most large areas," Lucas explained.

"Well, it is news to me. I never heard of such a thing. Actually, Lucas, what you're putting forward regarding the afterlife is sounding quite tame by comparison. People might be ready to accept your idea," said Andrew.

"It is a fact that when the soul crosses over, the soul doesn't care a fig about their old 'vehicle' left behind down here, or what happens to it. I think John Lennon had the best definition of death. When he was asked what death meant to him, he replied, 'leaving one vehicle and entering another vehicle!' Isn't that grand?" Marie smiled and clapped her hands.

Rosalie was having a great time. She had never been around such people before and she enjoyed hearing them express their beliefs. Her eyes danced as she sipped her tea.

"Simon, you've been very quiet. Anything you can add to the discussion?"

"It's odd: here I am, a clergyman who should be condemning you all to purgatory for your beliefs, yet I find myself quite comfortable in your company. Mind you, when I started out on my ministry, I was old school and would have had no part in all of this. But things changed. I joined the American Army as a chaplain, something every clergyman should do, and it opened my eyes to a different world. My experiences in war created a new side to my thinking. I discovered the true reasons we have wars and I found that terribly upsetting. I understood the reasoning of a draft dodger, and learned they were the only ones doing the right thing. I questioned much of what I was taught in university and seminary school. In actual fact an open mind would see that our beliefs are not at odds with orthodox religious teachings. Our beliefs and concepts run parallel to each other. The journey is the same; we just take different paths to reach the same destination," Simon said thoughtfully.

"Well said, Simon," said Lucas. I believe we are all questioning things we have been taught, learned, and experienced over the years right up to the present. Actually, there are more reasons to question now than ever! What about you, Marie. Any thoughts on the matter?"

"Lucas, I think back on our first meeting. You came for a reading and you were not fully committed to the whole idea of the afterlife and the soul thing, but you were searching. The expression on your face when you saw the light was priceless. Little did I know where our casual meeting would lead. And I'm proud to be a part of it. You know what? I would like to do a reading in court. Maybe the prosecutor. Or do a proxy sitting, a remote reading. Do you think that would be allowed?"

The men sat with their mouths open, eyes wide, stunned by Marie's suggestion. After they got over the shock, Lucas responded, "You know, that's not a bad idea. Really. Could you do it successfully in a crowded courtroom?"

"I don't see why not. I do group readings in auditoriums and I can read people successfully," Marie explained.

"What is this proxy sitting you mentioned?" Simon leaned forward, his interest showing.

"That's where the person having the reading is unknown to me. I have no idea who it is. All I have is their representative who comes in with his or her name. It really began as a test so the medium wouldn't be able to pick up clues on their demeanor or such. Like a validation of the medium being honest and above board," Marie said.

"A remote reading would really impress the jury. I'm pretty sure the judge would allow it. You might pick up something about the prosecutor, just in passing, maybe enough to give the jury a little laugh and embarrass him a little. That would be a hoot!" Andrew laughed and slapped his leg.

"Pass me the tin foil. I'm making me a hat," Simon said, laughing.

"How about you, Rosalie? Anything you want to say? I should tell you all, that, thanks to Ann, I had my first reading with Rosalie. You made me what I am today - I hope you're satisfied!" Lucas nodded fondly at Rosalie.

Rosalie laughed and looked around at the group.

"I don't really know how I can contribute to all this, Lucas. I don't understand all that I do half the time. I don't fault folks who laugh and make fun of what I do 'cause they don't understand and that's just how you act when you don't understand something. Being here today and listening to all the talk has given me new pride in what I do and I thank you for that, Lucas."

"No, Rosalie. Thank you for making me aware. I'm forever grateful," Lucas said sincerely. Then he looked around the group and said, "I think that just about does it folks. Tomorrow it starts. Ann and I would very much like to take everyone to supper tonight. Would your hotel be a good spot to eat, Simon?"

"What we've had there has been delightful. I'd recommend it," said Simon.

"All right then. The Westin it shall be. Marie, will you drop Simon off, please and thank you?

I've got to get my act together for tomorrow. Oh, what time tonight? Six, six thirty?" Lucas asked.

"Let's make it six, then we can get a good night's sleep, if we can sleep!" Andrew decided.

• • • • •

Everyone enjoyed the meal at the Westin. It was a relaxing evening with a lot of laughing and rather loud conversation. The group broke up early and went their separate ways. Rosalie had decided to accept Lucas' offer of staying over and the three of them got back to the house around eight thirty. It was just dark enough that Lucas didn't see a large black vehicle parked up the road from his house.

Ann decided to save time in the morning by having her shower before bed. Rosalie phoned her cousin and told him not to worry, that she was staying over and would be in good hands, but she asked his wife to pack an overnight bag. She gave her cousin specific directions on what to include and asked that this be delivered tomorrow morning. Then she checked out the den and her bed. Ann had laid out some sleeping garments for her.

Lucas took down what would be his 'suit of armor' for tomorrow's 'fight': everything black. Pants, socks, shoes, and bar vest. The white neck bands and tabs were hard to find but he managed to put everything together. He would carry the black robe.

After the ladies turned in, he went to the 'war room' to visit with Sarah. He looked longingly at her picture, wanting to hear her voice. He wished to hear her blessing on tomorrow knowing that she would be there. There were no more tears. His grief was given over to belief in an afterlife and that knowledge carried him now. As he studied every detail of her face, he silently asked her, 'How long before I can hold you again?' and a tear told a lie to the absence of grief. He finished his scotch and went to bed.

Everyone was up early the next morning. Lucas served scrambled eggs, tomatoes, and whole wheat toast with coffee and tea. There wasn't much conversation taking place and nervousness showed on their faces.

"How are you feeling, Lucas?" Ann asked. She usually enjoyed the first day of a trial, but this day was different. This wasn't just another trial. This one was groundbreaking, and if you weren't nervous you didn't see the big picture.

"I'm okay. Rosalie, will you be all right until Marie gets here? I'll turn the TV on for you. Or feel free to take a walk. It is a very safe area."

"Don't you worry about me, Lucas. I'll enjoy the new surroundings. It'll be a nice change."

"All right, then. I guess we're off to see the wizard. If we have time, Rosalie, we'll come back here for lunch. Wish us luck!"

$$\bullet \quad \bullet \quad \bullet \quad \bullet \quad \bullet$$

At the courthouse they were surprised to see the people waiting to get in to court. Press groups were represented also, even one or two from south of the border.

"It appears you have your audience," noted Ann.

"Exactly! This is what I was hoping for. I want as many people as possible to learn about what we are presenting. They don't have to believe it, but hopefully it will start them thinking," said Lucas.

Upon entering courtroom four, they saw that the small public seating area was already filled. The press was here too. Judge Muirhead had allowed two cameras which were set up on either side of the room, at the back so as not to be a distraction to witnesses. A low buzz of voices filled the air and particular attention was paid to Lucas as they walked to the front of the courtroom. Ann placed folders and notepads on the defence table to the left as Lucas took in the scene. Michael Sullivan and his team were in a huddle at their table. The court stenographer was checking her supplies and uncapping a bottle of water. The clerk was in his robe, waiting for the hands of his watch to tell him when to start proceedings. And there was the man in black in his usual seat. Lucas was concerned and wondered just what it was this man represented. Was he just an interested bystander or was there something more sinister involved here? His dress and presence certainly drew attention to himself but he appeared oblivious to the fact. Was he the driver of the black SUV that had followed them?

The door to the left of the judge's dias opened and Joseph Simpson was escorted to the defence table. Ann had done a good job in making him presentable. She got him to have a shave and haircut, a good suit, shirt, tie, shoes... even socks. He was a rendition of anybody's grandfather and he appeared to be enjoying himself. Even Michael Sullivan took notice of the transformation. The trustee removed the handcuffs and stood away to the left.

"Good morning, Joseph. Ready for your day in court? You're looking very dapper."

"Thank you, Miss Hughes. I'm as ready as I'll ever be, I guess. Hello, Mr. McNab."

"Good morning, Joseph. Have a seat. You're being treated well?"

"Treated quite well, Mr. McNab."

Just then the judge entered the courtroom and at the same time the bailiff gave the command, "All rise." Judge Muirhead, a brilliant red sash over his black robe, took his seat, signaling that the court could also sit. The judge was nearing eighty years of age and would soon be retiring. Lucas felt some remorse about him being the judge in this controversial trial. Lucas thought he didn't deserve this kind of trial. It could be his last.

The bailiff stood and stated that which he had done so many times.

"The Superior Court is now in session, Judge Arthur Muirhead presiding. The Crown verses Joseph Simpson. The charge is murder in the second degree. Will the accused please rise and face the court?"

Judge Muirhead looked sternly at Joseph and spoke: "Joseph Simpson, you are charged with murder in the second degree. Do you understand the charge?"

"I understand the charge, your Honour," said Joseph.

"And how do you plead to the charge?"

R.B. Brown

"I plead not guilty, your Honour."

"Take your seat, Mr. Simpson. Is the prosecution ready to proceed?"

"We are your Honour." Michael Sullivan and his pretty blond co-council stood as they answer the Judge.

"Is the defence ready to proceed?"

"Yes, we are, your Honour." Lucas and Ann also stood.

"Bailiff, bring in the jury," said the judge.

The jury entered in single file and took their seats in the jury box located along the wall to the right of the court.

"Has the jury chosen a foreman?"

The bailiff handed a paper to the judge who, upon reading it, addressed the chosen foreman. "Mr. Edward Thompson, you have been selected by your peers to be their foreman. Do you accept their decision?"

Thompson stood. "Yes, your Honour."

"Thank you, Mr. Thompson. You may proceed, Mr. Sullivan."

Sullivan eased over to the podium to the left of their table, turned, and addressed the jury with his opening remarks.

"Ladies and gentlemen of the jury. I want to thank you for your dedication and responsibility to our legal system. This trial is a murder trial and nothing more. We will place before you irrefutable evidence to the fact that the accused, Joseph Simpson, on the night of April 19 of this year, did willfully and in cold blood, murder one Charles Conlon, in the bandstand of the Public Gardens. You will also hear Mr. Simpson's confession, made that very night, excuse me, that next morning, to city police officers in which he describes how the murder was committed and why. The defence will present you with another completely different scenario, as is their right and obligation to the accused. I ask you to listen carefully to all the evidence presented to you, weigh it carefully on the scales of justice that each of you have in your mind. Do this, and you will come to the *only* conclusion that makes sense... *guilty as charged!* Thank you, ladies and gentlemen."

"Call your first witness, Mr. Sullivan" directed the judge.

"The prosecution calls Constable Robert Halliday to the witness stand."

"Constable Robert Halliday, come forward."

The courtroom door was opened by a security officer. Robert Halliday proceeded to the witness box where he was sworn in by the Bailiff.

"Constable Halliday, were you on the duty desk at the Gottingen Street detachment on the night in question?" The Crown got right to the job at hand.

"I was."

"Have you seen the accused before and, if so, under what circumstances?" Michael was turned toward the jury to direct their attention to the witness.

"He came in to the detachment admitting desk and said he had just killed someone in the Public Gardens. I recorded the time and it was 3:17 a.m. on April 20."

"That's pretty unusual even for Halifax. Did you believe him at the time?"

"I took his statement but I was skeptical. I had a patrol car go to the location and they found a body just where he said it was."

"And where was this location, Constable," Sullivan asked.

"The accused reported that it was the Public Gardens band stand," replied the Constable.

"And where was Mr. Simpson at this time?"

"I booked him and then took his wallet, belt, and shoelaces, the usual procedure, and then I had him placed in a holding cell at the detachment."

"What did you do next, Constable?"

"I contacted the morgue with the pertinent information so they would pick up the body."

"Was the body identified?" Sullivan turned to the jury.

"Not for quite a while, but later it was learned that the deceased was one Charles Conlon."

"Your Honour, the Crown enters Mr. Simpson's confession, duly witnessed by two police officers as evidence. Exhibit One, your Honour." Sullivan distributed copies to the Judge, the court and the defence

"Constable Halliday, would you please read the defendant's confession to the court? First, do you recognize it as being a typed version of the confession made to you by the defendant on the morning of April 20 of this year?"

"Yes sir, I do."

The constable, turning directly to the jury, proceeded to read the confession to the court, with the jury members listening intently.

"That's all, Constable. Thank you. Your witness, Mr. McNab."

Lucas stepped to the small stand and adjusted the microphone.

"Constable Halliday, could you tell if Mr. Simpson had been drinking?"

"I could smell alcohol on him, yes sir."

"With that suspicion did you make any effort to determine Mr. Simpson's blood alcohol level?"

"No sir. I did not."

The spectators were extremely quiet, either through interest in the proceedings or fear of Judge Muirhead. A couple of jurors tilted their heads in a questioning manner,

"Just one other minor question, Constable Halliday. At the time of Mr. Simpson's purported confession, was there a lawyer representing Mr. Simpson in attendance?"

"No sir, there was not."

"And why was that, Constable? The accused has the right to an attorney before any statements are to be taken, is that not so?"

"Yes sir, it is. We advised Mr. Simpson of his rights and he waived them, quite strongly I might add. Several officers witnessed this. I assumed that an accused also has the right to do what Mr. Simpson did."

"Was Mr. Simpson drunk or sober when he made this decision?"

"Like I said before, I could smell liquor on him but he appeared to have full faculties."

"Your Honour, the defence wishes to have Mr. Simpson's confession deemed inadmissible based upon Constable Halliday's testimony." Lucas had the full attention of the courtroom with that statement.

Judge Muirhead considered the request briefly.

"I have no more questions, your Honour." Lucas sat down and patted Ann's arm reassuringly.

"The confession stands in evidence, Mr. McNab. Mr. Sullivan, call your next witness."

Lucas took notice of some jury members with a quizzical look on their faces. He turned slightly and saw there appeared to be some questioning looks by the public also.

"The Crown calls Constable Bruce O'Brien to the stand."

There was low murmuring throughout the public seating as the officer made his way to the witness stand.

"Constable O'Brien, you were on patrol the night in question when you were instructed to respond to a reported murder at the Public Gardens, is that correct?" Michael Sullivan gained confidence with every question he asked.

"Yes sir."

"And did you find a body?"

"Yes sir, we did. The body was located in the bandstand. It was like he was laid out, like he would be in a coffin. Arms folded across his chest. We didn't find any weapon and we found no wounds on the body. There was an empty rum bottle placed under his head."

"Were you able to find any witnesses?" Michael continued.

"No sir. We could not find any witnesses."

"Thank you, Constable." Michael turned to Lucas with a look of superiority."Your witness."

Lucas smiled and went to the microphone.

"Constable, did you check the body for any signs of life? Check for a pulse? The carotid artery? Did you check for breathing? Did you check *anything*, Constable O'Brien?"

"No sir, we did not."

"You simply *assumed* Mr. Conlon was dead. Might he have been alive? There was evidence of heavy drinking. Might he have been comatose and not dead at all, at that time?"

"I don't know, sir. We responded to a murder scene and I guess we just took for granted that if it was a murder, the victim would be dead... sir."

Lucas, feeling slightly foolish over the constable's answer could also hear soft snickering from the public seating.

"No further questions." Lucas took his seat at the defense table

"Call your next witness, Mr. Sullivan." Judge Muirhead was moving his trial right along.

"The Crown calls Dr. Henry Farmer."

The good doctor plodded up the carpeted aisle, through the gate and plopped down in the witness chair.

Michael Sullivan again made sure the jury members were concentrating on his questions by drawing attention to himself as much as possible.

"Dr. Farmer, you are the city coroner, correct?"

"That is correct."

"And how long have you held that position?"

"I've been coroner for seventeen years." Farmer seemed somewhat uncomfortable in the witness chair. He might have found it a bit small.

"And did you do a post-mortem on a male body on the 19th or 20th of April?"

"Yes, I did. I remember because it was the only one all that week."

" Were you aware of the situation regarding that body?"

" Yes I was made aware of the purpose of the autopsy and who it was."

"What did your autopsy reveal, Doctor?"

"It was difficult to determine the cause of death. There were no wounds of any kind. I did find fibres in the lungs which would point to suffocation. That was as close as I could come to determining a cause of death. I did discover that the body was ravaged by cancer which would have been causing the deceased great pain. He wouldn't have had long to live by my estimation."

Michael entered the autopsy report as evidence.

"Thank you, Doctor. No further questions."

"Mr. McNab?" the Judge queried Lucas.

"I have no questions, your Honour."

"That is all Doctor. Thank you," the judge waited until the doctor left the witness stand.

"Call your next witness Mr. Sullivan," said the judge, somewhat wearily.

"The Crown calls Reverend George Mumford."

Reverend Mumford walked quickly to the front of the court and sat in the witness box with a demeanor that gave the appearance of presiding over the Inquisition.

"Good morning, Reverend."

"Good morning to you."

"Where do you minister and how long have you been there as pastor?"

"I am pastor of the Church of Everlasting Light in Lower Sackville and have had the great privilege of ministering to the good people of Lower Sackville for nearly twenty years. It was through my determination that we were able to erect our church. The congregation of the Church of Everlasting Light are truly a wonderful, God-fearing group of people!"

"I'm sure they are, Reverend, but let us move on. What does the Bible tell us about having a soul and an afterlife?" Michael sensed he had just loaded a canon all he had to do was duck when it went off.

"You may ask, 'what is a soul?' The soul isn't just a separate part within man. The soul represents a living person. You do not *have* a soul, you *are* a soul. 'And the Lord God formed man of the dust of the ground and breathed into his nostrils the breath of life, and man became a living soul; Genesis 2, verse 7. Now, what happens to the soul when we die? The soul is no more. The Bible says, in Ecclesiastes

12, verse 7, 'Then the dust will return to the earth as it is, and the spirit will return to God who gave it.'"

The reverend was in church and his congregation was spread out before him. He could feel the spirit welling up inside. 'Don't stop me now!' he thought.

"You might wonder 'What is this spirit that returns to God?' The spirit is the breath of life it refers to in Job 27, verse 3: 'All the while my breath is in me, and the spirit of God is in my nostrils.' Can the soul die? Yes, it can… and it does, because the soul is a living person, and persons die. Souls, or human beings, cannot live on after they die. Only God has immortality. The Bible says that very thing in Timothy 6, verses 15 and 16. When we die there is no soul or spirit that continues to exist on Earth or anywhere else. Once again, in Ecclesiastes 9, verses 5 and 6: 'For the living know that they will die, but the dead know nothing and they have no reward for the memory of them is forgotten.' All emotions cease at…!"

Lucas turned in his chair and noticed several pairs of hands in the air. He blinked in astonishment.

"Thank you, Reverend. You cleared that up very nicely. And now, can you tell us what the Bible says about heaven?" Now, duck!

Reverend Mumford could barely keep himself seated. He wanted to jump up and shout 'Hallelujah!!'

"You may search the Bible for proof of any kind that indicates that we go to heaven when we die, and you will not find any. I have searched the Bible through and could not find any such proof. In Luke 23, verse 43, it says, 'Jesus said to him', the thief on the cross that is, 'Jesus said to him, you will be with me in Paradise.' Now, you have to understand the biblical use of the word, Paradise. It actually means an enclosed garden or a park-like setting. It was used in reference to the Garden of Eden also."

Lucas was listening to the reverend and making notes. He was also carefully reviewing what reference material Simon Harris had given him.

"Thank you, Reverend. That's fine…"

"You must understand. God is coming *here*, not people going to heaven. There is no knowledge of anything beyond the grave. Death is like a sleep, and at the resurrection God will awaken all from their sleep for something far better than heaven and hell..."

Michael interrupted the pastor once again. "Thank you, Pastor Mumford. That is all." He turned to Lucas with raised eyebrows. "Your witness, Mr. McNab."

"Good morning, Reverend. I won't keep you here much longer. What is your interpretation of the following, taken from Genesis 1, verse 26: 'Then God said, let *us* make man in *our* image, according to *our* likeness.' Now, to a layman like myself, I read this and it sounds as if God is leading a delegation of some sort, perhaps a landing party from some other galaxy or a group of beings not of this Earth, preparing to populate it with beings designed by committee..."

Michael rose quickly to his feet. "Your Honour! I strongly object to council's question! It has absolutely *nothing* to do with this trial and certainly nothing to do with this witness's testimony."

"Sustained. The jury will disregard the defence's last question."

"I apologize your Honour." Lucas continued, "Pastor Mumford, you stated that there is no heaven to which the dead ascend, is that correct?"

"That is correct. At the resurrection God will come to Earth and all will dwell on a new earth. It will become, in fact, a heaven on Earth!"

"That's fine pastor. But explain the following from John 14, verses 1 to 3: 'Let not your heart be troubled, you believe in God, believe also in me. In my father's house are many mansions; if it were not so I would have told you. *I go to prepare a place for you.*' Lucas read the last with as much drama as he could muster. "What do you think that means, Reverend?"

"I... I believe the Bible when it states that the righteous do not go to heaven when they die. They are only asleep in their graves and Jesus will return and raise them up to immortal life. It says this in Corinthians 15, verses 50 to 57."

"You also testified that the Bible states that we don't have a soul, that we are souls, that the soul is a living person and that the soul dies with the body. Correct?"

"That is correct."

"In Genesis 35, verse 18, regarding the death of Rachael: 'And so it was as her soul was *departing*.' And there is this taken from Psalm 146, verse 4: 'His spirit *departs*, he returns to his earth in that very day his plans perish.'

"And this from Matthew 16, verse 26: 'What good will it be for someone to gain the whole world, yet forfeit their *soul*!'

"This from Psalm 62, verse 1: 'Truly my *soul* finds rest in God...'

"And here, from John 1, verse 2: 'Dear friend, I pray that you may enjoy good health and that all may go well with you, even as your *soul* is getting along well.'"

"Yes... but... but..."

"I have no more questions of this witness, your Honour."

Looking at the faces of the jury Lucas sensed they were evaluating the good reverend's testimony as he walked quickly from the court room.

Michael had just experienced Lucas pull the fuse out of the canon.

"Call your next witness, Mr. Sullivan."

"The Crown calls Dr. Sidney Overstreet."

Overstreet took the stand.

"Good morning, Doctor. You have a PhD in applied science, is that correct?"

"That is correct. I attended Saint Mary's University here in the city."

"And tell the court a brief history of your work after graduating."

"Certainly. I was employed at the University of Westchester in Ohio for fifteen years where I conducted research related to muscular degeneration in the elderly. While there I was also visiting professor to numerous higher educational institutions involved in researching the aging process in humans."

"That's very impressive. Would you please explain what you do as an applied physicist?"

"Applied physics is the application of the science of physics to help human beings and solve their problems. Applied physicists use physics, or conduct physics research, to develop new technologies in this regard."

"Doctor Overstreet, during your extensive work with the elderly, did you ever witness any evidence of the existence of a person's soul? Anything that might have caused you to consider the possibility of there being a soul?"

"As you know, the older we get the more important the implications of death become, on a personal level. I have heard the term used as an expression of endearment, particularly among the elderly. 'She's such a dear soul', 'Poor soul', and other expressions like that."

"To the best of your knowledge have you ever heard any colleagues mention the possibility of there being a human soul?"

"I suspect we have all used the term in comments referring to traits of particular personalities, such as, 'He has a good soul', or 'He doesn't have a soul', expressions of that nature. It appears we use the term without thought of the meaning, just the same as we say 'He has a good head on his shoulders.'"

"I'm sure you have had working relationships with medical doctors of various disciplines. Have you ever heard them mention a soul or refer to a soul?" Michael turned to the jury.

"No, I have not. Considering that surgeons have the closest contact with the human body, you would think they would be the first to declare the fact. To my knowledge this has never happened."

"Do you understand the meaning of soul?"

"I am aware of the word as it is used in musical lyrics and poetry and my previous reference. It occurs to a limited extent in the Bible, but I don't believe any scientist has been able to 'isolate' a 'soul'. Humanity has to abandon these fanciful beliefs and focus on what the laws of the universe dictate. The laws of physics underlying everyday life are completely understood and within these laws there really isn't anything that would allow any form of consciousness to exist after death. The very concept of life after death would, without a doubt, require physics far beyond that practiced now."

Michael showed a smug smile as he slowly turned to the jury.

"Have you any knowledge of an 'afterlife'?"

"I have heard the elderly talk of going to heaven. I don't recall hearing the term 'afterlife'. We have been told about heaven since childhood and it stands to reason that as we age, entering heaven would occupy our thoughts more and more."

"Now, Doctor, I'm going to ask you your opinion on 'near-death experiences', NDEs as they're called. What can you tell us about these? They are closely linked to both the 'soul' and the 'afterlife', as I understand."

"I have not done research on NDEs per se, but I have read about them, just out of curiosity. I believe there is some research being conducted and I can give you pertinent results from that research if you like."

"That would be fine, Doctor. Please continue."

"First, let me make clear that not everyone who enters a near-death state reports an NDE. Many do not. Now, research has found that stress releases endorphins. This is a 'feel good' hormone something akin to morphine. It can give a patient a feeling of peace and love. Also, excess carbon dioxide in the blood can affect vision and could result in the tunnel or bright light often reported. It is well known that oxygen deprivation can cause hallucinations and could explain a feeling of euphoria. Spikes in brain activity might result in sensory perceptions and improved clarity also experienced. Reactions to anaesthetics, Cortazan for example, can trigger out-of-body experiences and hallucinations."

Lucas had to admit that Overstreet was doing an excellent job, showing complete confidence in all of his answers. No hesitation whatever. He might be a tough nut to crack.

Jury members were nodding their heads in apparent agreement with Overstreet's testimony. The public too seemed impressed with the doctor.

"Thank you, Dr. Overstreet. Your answers have enlightened us all, I am sure."

"Does the defence wish to cross-examine this witness?" asked Judge Muirhead.

"I do, your Honour," answered Lucas.

"Good morning, Dr. Overstreet. I won't keep you much longer. There are just a few points I wish to address. In your testimony regarding NDEs I counted four 'cans', two 'coulds', and one 'might'. Now Doctor, those powerful little words don't instill a lot of confidence in the research being conducted. In fact, it would appear that it is mere supposition and not research at all! In fact, Doctor, it doesn't constitute legitimate evidence at all, wouldn't you agree?"

Lucas continued quickly, not giving the witness a chance to respond.

The jury, all ears now, were leaning forward to catch Lucas' attempt to shoot down Doctor Overstreet's testimony.

"Now, about the so-called research into anaesthetics and possible reactions to them. You state that Cortazan *can*, oops! There's another one, *can* trigger out of body experiences and more hallucinations and even frightening dreams. My research indicates that Cortazan is used as a local for minor surgeries and it is an experimental drug being tested for weight loss. Did your research discover that, Doctor? I have no more questions, your Honour."

Ann couldn't read the jury with this witness. She thought Michael could have won this round.

"Mr. Sullivan, does the Crown have witnesses for this afternoon? asked Judge Muirhead.

"No, your Honour. The Crown rests its case."

"We will break for lunch and resume at two this afternoon. Will the defence be ready to proceed at that time?"

Lucas stood. "We will, your Honour."

"Court is now in recess until two this afternoon."

• • • • •

As the members of the public made their way out of the courtroom, Lucas noticed that the man in black was already gone. The press sharks were getting ready to circle the Crown team. Lucas knew his turn would come this afternoon. He and Ann escaped through a side entrance and made their way to Lucas' car. Since it was only noon they decided to head to the house.

When they arrived, they found that everyone was there in seemingly good spirits, eager to learn of the progress of the trial.

"Quick! Tell us! How did it go?" Marie enthusiastically posed the question.

"Lucas did a great job on cross-examinations! It was like shooting clay pigeons. Sullivan would throw them up and Lucas would shoot 'em down. It was quite a show, believe you me," Ann exclaimed. She went on to explain her shooting gallery in more detail as Lucas poured a coffee.

"How are you making out, Rosalie? Finding everything okay?" Lucas asked.

"Oh, yes, Lucas. Marie and me are having a grand old time, and I'm learning so much. It has just been wonderful. My cousin dropped off a suitcase of my things so I'm doing just fine. Marie made up some 'samwitches' for you and Ann. Make sure you eat something now."

Lucas took Andrew Cushing aside and explained the afternoon session to him. He gave a rundown of Overstreet's testimony and what he planned to cover with him on the stand.

"I don't think we should be too worried about the Crown's cross-examination. They'll be looking for chinks to exploit but we won't leave them any. I'll put you on the stand first, Andrew. The last testimony the jury heard was their science guy so I want to counter whatever they remember about his testimony. Okay?"

"Whatever you say, Lucas. I'm looking forward to the experience."

"I'll be gentle since its your first time!" And they both laughed.

Next, Lucas took Simon Harris aside and explained the afternoon to him. "Simon, we have to be careful with the jury. You know the old story about religion and politics..."

"They don't mix and don't argue them," quipped Simon.

"That's right. It appears to be a responsible jury so if we treat them with respect I think we'll be respected, even though what we cover will be at odds with what some of them have been brought up thinking. I'll keep it effective but easy to understand... I hope!" Turning now to Marie, Lucas said, "Marie, we'll get together this evening and map out our strategy for tomorrow morning. And I can't thank you enough for all you've done. I'm afraid I've taken you for granted, but know it wasn't on purpose. I promise you that tomorrow will be worth all your efforts and then some!."

Lucas gave Marie a long hug and a kiss on the cheek. Ann didn't see it.

"Rosalie, I think you should be at court tomorrow morning with Marie. Will that be alright with you?" Lucas asked.

"Certainly, Lucas, that's why I'm here," Rosalie responded.

Lucas was too nervous to eat much. He noticed Ann was only nibbling too. It was getting close to the time to leave and he got the two men ready. They both seemed calm enough and that eased Lucas' concerns somewhat.

• • • • •

At the courthouse they walked their two witnesses to the hall where they would wait to be called. He smiled, wished them good luck, and shook their hands. They made their way to the defense table past the press with their questions. Michael Sullivan was shuffling through papers. He looked over at Lucas and nodded. Lucas caught a look on Michael's face that was not one of confidence. Instead, it was a look of concern. 'Concern for what?' Lucas wondered.

The usual preliminaries over, Judge Muirhead addressed Lucas. "Is the defense ready to proceed?"

"We are, your Honour," Lucas answered.

"Call your first witness, Mr. McNab."

"The defence calls Dr. Andrew Cushing to the stand."

Andrew entered court and walked with a reserved bearing to the witness box where he was sworn in by the bailiff.

"Good afternoon, Dr. Cushing. Would you tell the court where you obtained your doctorate, please?"

"My doctorate was obtained from the Imperial College in London, UK."

"The Imperial College is consistently ranked among the top universities in the world, is it not?"

"It is." Andrew sat back and crossed his legs. The jury noted his demeanor

"And what is your field of learning, Doctor?"

"I have my PhD in advanced aeronautical engineering."

"Please tell us what it was that triggered your interest and research in the afterlife."

"I had a very serious illness in... 1995. For three days I was in a coma. At a point during this time I was acknowledged by doctors as being clinically dead for several minutes. During those minutes I experienced an NDE, a near-death experience."

Lucas noted the intense interest shown by the jury as Andrew spoke.

"Can you describe what you experienced during your NDE?"

"Yes. I suddenly found myself hovering above the bed watching the doctors and nurses working feverishly to save my life. I could hear their panic; I watched as they brought equipment into the room; I saw myself with tubes and equipment everywhere. I floated around the room just under the ceiling..."

"You must have been scared to death, Doctor!"

"Scared? I was petrified! I couldn't understand what was happening to me! Suddenly, I was outside the hospital, really high. I saw a bird's nest on a window ledge of a top floor window. I heard a voice from somewhere saying my name and telling me, 'Go back, go back! This is not your time'... and I returned to my body. Shortly thereafter I came out of my coma and began my convalescence. I told the doctors about my out-of-body experience and seeing the bird's nest. They actually searched for that nest and they found it... exactly where I had told them it would be. That was the proof of my NDE because you could not see the nest from ground level."

Ann noted the jury seemed mesmerized by Andrew's experience.

"And this experience resulted in your interest in NDEs and consequently the afterlife?"

"It certainly did. It wasn't immediately after, mind you. It evolved over a period of several months."

"And what was your approach to your research?"

"I would have to say that my education set me on a scientific path in my search for answers. I researched both pros and cons of the paranormal from various sources."

"Dr. Cushing, I ask you now to tell the court the details of your research, in general parameters of course, and your conclusion regarding the afterlife."

It was now Lucas' turn to court the jury. He turned them over to Andrew and they were his.

"Certainly. Since my first experience with the paranormal was my NDE, I started there. I learned that there were thousands, some estimate millions of persons worldwide who have reported having NDEs. Many of these have been chronicled by various paranormal researchers and most, if not all, have been accepted as fact. Naturally, not all have been investigated scientifically. One search led to another and soon I was delving into other areas of the so-called paranormal. My main interest, naturally, was the role of science in all of this. I anticipated a negative attitude because of the parameters set out by the physics community. And there was some negativity, but I was pleasantly surprised by the number and quality of the many scientists who at least had an open mind. I made a list of some of these scientists. Shall I read them to the court?"

"By all means, Doctor."

As Andrew read off the list, Lucas kept a watchful eye on the jury. He didn't want to lose them in a lot of scientific mumbo-jumbo. He thought they still showed interest. He entered Andrew's list into evidence.

"Please continue, Doctor."

"I discovered that there is an awakening in the scientific field, a revolution if you will. Our approach to phenomena such as NDE must be included but is presently being ignored to some extent. I will say that as a group, physicists are questioning what we take to be reality and admit to the possibility of other worlds including an afterlife. Science has always been close-minded and outdated. Here's an example: Professor Simon Newcomb boldly stated that 'it was *scientifically impossible for machines to fly.*' At the time he was referring to the efforts of the Wright brothers! We have come a long way from that type of thinking!"

The mention of the Wright Brothers brought forth smiles from the jury.

"Thank you, Doctor. During your research did you find any noted scientists who have been receptive to the idea of an afterlife?"

"Yes, I did."

"Would you tell the court who these scientists are, please."

Andrew read off a short list of earlier scientists such as Max Plank, Swedenburg and others.

" And although not a scientist, Sir Winston Churchill admitted to having past lives, which he believed prepared him for his role during World War II. And, of course, we have heard of the stories of our Prime Minister MacKenzie King seeking advice from his deceased mother."

"That certainly is an impressive list of afterlife believers. Dr. Cushing, for the average person who is learning of the afterlife for the first time, could you please explain in simple terms what actually takes place when we pass on?"

Michael Sullivan rose quickly to his feet.

"Your Honour, the Crown strongly objects! The defence is presenting evidence that is leading this trial nowhere. Mr. McNab has forgotten that this is a murder trial. To this point I have no idea what it is he's defending!"

"Your Honour, if learned council for the Crown would check transcripts of his witnesses, he will find that I am only expanding on what was presented as a result of his own questioning."

Judge Muirhead looked over the papers in front of him.

"I'm afraid he's correct, Mr. Sullivan. Objection overruled. Continue, Mr. McNab."

"Thank you, your Honour. The question, Doctor, was can you explain, in simple terms, what happens when we pass on?"

"Yes. Well, I'll use an analogy. Let's compare the human body to a car. They both serve the same purpose, that being transportation. Both require energy to run, and this energy needs fuel to keep it going. In the case of the car we 'feed' it gasoline, oil, and lubrication. We feed our body vegetables, fruit, water, and a lot of junk our energy *doesn't* require. Now, if we don't 'feed' the car properly, after a while it quits running. We take it to a 'hospital' and the 'doctor' there says we're too late and the car dies. It ends up in a scrap heap somewhere, perhaps gets recycled into another car. If we stop feeding our bodies they too will stop functioning. It is not the heart, lungs, and other organs alone that give us life. It is our energy bodies that make them all work. Our energy body, our soul, sustains our physical body just like the car is 'sustained' by the fuel we give it. We dispose of our old carcass by burying it in the ground or we burn it. If we're really stupid, we freeze it in the hope of being thawed out when a repair kit is found for whatever killed the body. But, just like the car we get 'recycled' into a new body too, because our soul is pure energy and energy can't be destroyed. So, where does the soul go? To the afterlife is where.

"Try to think of it this way: If you are in a horrendous car accident, both 'vehicles' are totalled, the metal car and your body, but you, your soul, will survive and return 'home' - to the afterlife."

Lucas kept an eye on the jurors during Andrew's analogy. It was a masterful presentation, he thought, and the jury was transfixed.

"Thank you, Dr. Cushing. That was a telling analogy. We hear the term energy used frequently when discussing the soul. What can you tell us about our energy?"

"The new science accepts the fact that the universe, and ourselves, are made up of energy, not matter as Sir Isaac Newton made the world believe. Socrates believed in energy and it was accepted in India before that. Socrates said that our energy, which is our soul, is separate from matter. He believed that the whole universe was energy. The law of conservation of energy states that energy is neither created nor destroyed. Each and every one of us is energy and we are not very efficient at using our energy either. It is estimated that the human body is less than five per cent efficient."

"Now, Dr. Cushing, we come to the soul. What did your research tell you about the soul?"

The jury, as one, leaned forward to hear Andrew's testimony.

"Research showed me unequivocally that we all have a soul. This can not be debated. It is an accepted fact whether we realize it or not.

The soul is our energy as I explained earlier and cannot be destroyed. It goes on forever, giving us eternal life. It is not our brain or our mind that defines a person; it is our soul. Other than that, I can enlighten the court no further."

"That's fine, Dr. Cushing. Thank you. I will ask you this last question and please think carefully before you answer. As a result of all your research what is your considered opinion regarding the crime of murder?"

Andrew followed Lucas' advice and took a long pause before answering. Finally, he turned to the jury. "Based upon my research regarding the soul I have to say... I don't believe it is possible to commit murder."

There was a court-wide gasp. The jurors were stunned. The members of the press ran around like headless chickens. Judge Muirhead rapped his gavel in an attempt to bring back order to his trial.

"Order! Order!" The judge kept barking and banging.

Lucas looked over at the prosecution table. Michael looked subdued. His head was bowed and his hands were clasped just in front of his face. He appeared in supplication.

Ann took Lucas by the arm. They looked questioningly at each other. Then they both looked at Joseph who had turned in his chair to watch the commotion. Lucas leaned close to Ann's ear. "We won't be able to escape the hordes today, I'm afraid."

After several minutes the sound of the judge's gavel was heard above the din and a semblance of order was restored.

"Another display like that and I will empty the courtroom!" stated the judge. "Are you finished with your witness, Mr. McNab?"

"Yes, your Honour, I am."

"Do you wish to cross-examine, Mr. Sullivan?"

"No, your Honour." Michael's voice was quiet.

"You may step down, Dr. Cushing. The defence will call their next witness."

"The defence calls Reverend Simon Harris."

As Simon entered court, the man in black quickly slipped out before the door closed.

Great anticipation was shown throughout the courtroom because of the initial bombshell by the defence witness. Everyone expected bigger and better explosions from subsequent witnesses. The murmurs sounded like a soft breeze blowing through leaves on trees. Judge Muirhead heard it and tapped his gavel several times.

"I remind all of you of my warning. Quiet in the court."

Simon was sworn in and took his seat in the witness chair. He and Lucas exchanged the usual pleasantries preceding Lucas' first question.

"I understand you have a doctorate, Reverend. Please tell the court where you obtained your doctorate and in which discipline."

"I attended Embry College in Bakersfield, California graduating from their department of religion with courses in comparative religions, religious cultures, ethics in society, religious historical studies, and theological studies, to name a few."

"We have been listening to testimony from both the Crown and the defence regarding the soul and the afterlife. You have studied the soul from a religious point of view, I believe. Would you please tell the court what you have learned about the soul?"

"I'm pleased to share what I have learned from my research into the soul. I have to say my questioning began at a very early age, in Sunday school."

A snicker floated quickly throughout the court. Smiling jury members nudged each other.

"In Sunday school we would be taught wonderful parables of Jesus and the wonderful person he was and how bountiful and loving was God. We would march back up to our front pew singing our little hearts out on 'Jesus Wants Me for A Sunbeam', and then we would sit and listen to the minister talk about fire and brimstone, hell and damnation. There was something wrong with this picture and it scared me, which was the minister's intent. I became a victim of the old fear-based religion. To this day, to say a person is 'God-fearing' is perceived as a great compliment. Here's a scoop for those people: there is no trick to being God-fearing.

"We are a society that takes very little for granted, and that is a good thing. As a result, we look for proof of a soul. That was the basis of my research. What proof, if any, did I come up with? Here is a fact; I discovered there are hundreds of books, perhaps thousands worldwide, written positively regarding the soul, yet I could not find one, not one, written against the existence of the soul. That fact alone is quite telling."

Lucas noticed the court was appropriately quiet as a church. No one dared to miss a word from this witness. The press was practically drooling in anticipation.

"There are thousands upon thousands of near-death experiences recorded and verified. These people were so near to death that it took tremendous effort to bring them back to life. They are now living proof of a soul. Their souls left their physical bodies and were making their way back 'home'. Many made it to the afterlife and were able to describe what they saw. Disbelievers try their best to find logical, scientific-based explanation for these NDEs, some of which become so convoluted that you just shake your head in disbelief. All of their interpretations are sheer guesswork and none have been proven. I often think what would happen if one of these skeptics had an NDE. I would love to talk to them after. Wouldn't that be interesting?

"I will now discuss the mediums and psychics that I researched. For the most part, these are gifted persons who are able to communicate with souls of those departed of this earthly life and convey messages to those still here. As in any endeavour involving people you will run into fakes and scam artists. You expect that. Going back hundreds of years there were more fakes than honest clairvoyants, and it is because of this, I believe, that a lot of people still are skeptical of the process. I'll go out on a limb and say that debunkers have not had a session with a certified medium. They personify that old saying: 'if you can't see it, it doesn't exist.' Mediums have been an accepted part of various societies for thousands of years. Mediums and psychics might just be the crucial factor in the revived interest in the soul of man and the afterlife."

Lucas saw the jury showing continued interest in Simon's testimony, but something about Michael's demeanor was troubling. He seemed distracted and removed from the trial.

"There has always been an innate belief in the dead going on to another place. Our earliest ancestors might not have known anything about a soul but they had a belief in an afterlife. We have seen how the pharaohs were interred with all sorts of articles they would need in their afterlife. That's only one example Somewhere down the line, the soul comes into play and it is clearly associated with the way we conduct our lives and our reception in the afterlife. For example, Corinthians 15, verses 42 to 44: 'There is a *natural body* and a *spiritual body*. And we can find proof of a soul further back in time. The following is attributed to King Solomon who died in 931, BC: 'Your own soul is nourished when you are kind, it is destroyed when you are mean.'

"Then we have this from Plato, the Greek philosopher and founder of the first institution of higher learning in the Western world: 'Have you ever sensed that our soul is immortal and never dies?' So you see, the soul is nothing new. It was recognized as being an important part of ourselves centuries ago. All religions have a higher deity that they have faith in. We talk about having faith in God, faith in a second coming, and so on. Faith is just belief without proof. Yet, when we talk about the soul or the afterlife, we demand proof. And lots of it! I overheard some reporters talking about a comparison that had been made between a car and our body. I can't think of a more direct and clear comparison of what happens to us.

"My research has proved beyond a doubt that we have a soul and it is what makes us a person. Granted, science cannot definitively prove the soul, but it is understood that the soul is what defines you as a person and is responsible in large part for your personality. I believe we are here on a mission and the mission is known to the soul. Answer this question: if you knew you couldn't fail, how would you live your life? Try and find your soul's mission. When you do, follow it and experience the joy and purpose that is your right. I would like to add that I sense our souls are being subjected to terrorism every day. The evil in the world today can take your wealth, your car and property, your health and strength, your friends and family, but they *cannot take your soul.* You would have to surrender your soul up to evil."

"Thank you, Reverend Harris, for that most interesting and thoughtful testimony. And what about the afterlife?"

"All right. We know the soul and we know it is immortal, so what happens to it after the body dies? Where does it go? Most religious beliefs and concepts of the afterlife, such as descriptions of heaven preferred by Judaism, Christianity, and Islam, are simply articles of faith, to be accepted without having or asking for evidence or proof. The scientific quest for the answer to immortality, however, is based on the belief that evidence is not only necessary but, in fact, already exists in the form of NDEs, mediums, psychics, and others.

"The afterlife is another astral plane. The soul, like ET, goes home, in our case to the Source, or you may say God. Every sect has their own name for it. It is the place where souls begin their journey and return upon graduating from this earthly schoolroom. There are some societies that party for days when a loved one passes. It is like celebrating a graduation from high school. Like parents seeing their child off on their own path after graduation, they are sad to see them go, not knowing when they will see them again. This is their grief."

Reverend Harris' silence indicated he was through.

"Thank you again, Reverend. Before you leave I have one last question for you."

Here it comes. Everyone held their breath, watching and listening with their eyes and ears wide open. Lucas again looked directly at the jury.

"Reverend Harris, in your opinion… is it possible for the accused to have murdered Charles Conlon?"

The spectators could barely contain themselves. Judge Muirhead had his gavel poised and ready. Simon also took a long pause before answering. He turned to face the jury.

"The body... yes. The person... no!"

"Thank you, Reverend Harris."

The spectators were more subdued this time. Some were reacting as if they had won a bet. The press corps, knowing the day was over, left the courtroom and jockeyed for camera position outside.

• • • • •

The man in black sat in his parked vehicle and watched the tide of humanity flood out of the Law Courts building. He watched to see how the Crown attorney acted with the press. He appeared reserved, just as he should. There was no indication that the defence team was going to show. The press had the whole story anyway. He reached into the glove box, took out the dedicated phone, and reached his contact in Ottawa.

"Hello. Defence put their first two witnesses on this afternoon. They were very effective. The jury seemed impressed. He is doing well. Your concerns were well-founded. I would say tomorrow will be the last day of the trial so I will initiate the measures at once. Nothing has changed in that regard, I take it?"

"You are correct. Nothing has changed. Reports are coming in from around the world. It is starting to catch on, I'm afraid. Our southern friends are quite upset and threatened to take care of matters themselves. Whatever it takes, the trial must never reach the hands of the jury. Remember too that your actions must never be traced. Do what you have to do and then vanish. Accidents all the way. You are aware of the assets we have set up down there. Don't hesitate to use them. We are depending on your judgement as to who will be affected. Everything depends on you. This will be your last call so dispose of the phone. Remember, leave no clues. Good luck."

• • • • •

Important encounters are planned by the souls
long before the bodies see each other.
Paul Coelho

As they left the court, Lucas turned to Ann.

"Tonight, we use your apartment. The press will be at my house in full force. We should have packed something for tomorrow. Gentlemen, you were tremendous! You got the message out loud and clear. Simon, you can call your good wife when we get to the apartment. Andrew, I have to call Marie anyway so we can let her know. I'm sure Ann will have some celebratory wine at her place, won't you?"

"We'll find something. How do you think your testimony came across, Andrew?" Ann asked.

"I didn't want to get too scientific with the jury. That can really turn folks off in a hurry. I tried to keep it basic and simple and I think I achieved that. What would you say, Lucas?"

"I think it was beautifully done. I kept one eye on the jury and they were hanging on your every word. How about you, Simon? What grade would you give yourself?"

"B+. It was most difficult not to preach our beliefs and avoid being contentious. My wish is that I presented the ideas in a fashion that will interest them enough to do more research on their own. There could be some very interesting sermons come Sunday!"

"Well, I think you did a masterful presentation, Simon. Just a great job. I thank you both from my heart ... and *soul*! and Lucas joined in on the laughter.

The SUV filled with tension-releasing laughter at Simon's comment.

Ann's apartment area was clear of people and cars, though they weren't sure for how long. The three men stood around in the little kitchen, still too buoyed up from the afternoon. Ann found wine and served glasses to everyone. Lucas made the toast.

"To a new awakening. May it serve to bring peace in our time."

"That wasn't very original," Ann chided. "Remember what happened to the last man who proudly proclaimed that?"

"Yeah? Well that was then and this is now!" Lucas put his arm around Ann's neck. "Let's make some calls. Simon, you first."

Simon reached his wife and told her where he was and all about the trial. He said that would be back shortly.

Lucas called Marie with the same news but added he wanted to see her that evening.

"Is the press over there, Marie?"

"There are quite a few reporters, Lucas, but they're behaving themselves. Rosalie and I are doing okay. Don't worry. I'm not sure how we're going to manage to get together though."

"I'll come up with something. Don't you and Rosalie drink all my scotch, now."

Ann had managed to put together a tray of snacks and they all found seats between the kitchen and the living room. The adrenaline was dissipating and Simon and Andrew were more relaxed. Although their part in the trial was over, Lucas still felt responsible for them while in the city. He knew what the results of the trial would mean to a great number of people. He knew that you should never step on the tail of a rattlesnake, but he just had. The presence of the man in black kept gnawing at him.

"I'm going to be frank with you, Simon, Andrew. You know what I've done and you can be sure there will be repercussions from many quarters. I'm forever in your debt. Simon, I have the feeling you might be looking for a place to settle in our little province. Is that true?"

"I'll admit we have given it some thought. The girls are quite taken with the beauty and the friendliness of the people, as am I. Why do you ask, Lucas?"

"Simon, I am advising you to rent a car tomorrow morning and take your family out of the city. Go explore the rest of the province. You have my number. Call anytime to keep up with events. Promise me you will do that. Promise?"

"If you think that's what we should do, certainly. I promise."

"Thank you, Simon. Andrew, after tomorrow morning Marie's name will be known, and her address will quickly follow, so I wouldn't be long in leaving the city. And take Marie with you. I don't know anything more than that. I'm reacting to a hunch… and a feeling in my soul. Rosalie will be fine. Her cousin will pick her up and no man, in any colour suit, would survive making a threat in Prospect. There, I think I've covered all the bases."

"Not quite, I'm afraid. What about yourself and Ann?" Andrew looked concerned.

"Andrew's right, Lucas," Simon agreed. "You know you're the one going to take the brunt of any reaction, you and Ann. What are your plans?"

Lucas looked longingly at Ann. Watching his face she moved to his side and put her arm around his waist.

"We'll go somewhere safe until interest wanes. We'll be okay; don't worry about us. We both want to tell you how proud we are to have met you all. I only wish it could have been under more pleasant and happier circumstances. But be assured, you are part of something that has real meaning to a lot of people, I hope. Do take care. We've started something much bigger than we realize. Simon, I'll call you that taxi, and please pass on our pleasure in meeting Virginia and your lovely daughter Rebecca. Give them our love and best wishes."

As Simon was leaving for the taxi Lucas slipped an envelope of money into his jacket pocket.

• • • • •

Lucas knew they had to go to the house. He wouldn't be able to duck the press any longer. Might as well get it over with. They were all apprehensive on the drive, with no one saying much. They were startled to see the crowd of people milling around the front lawn. The anxious mob turned into hungry chickens as the SUV turned into the driveway.

"I'll get out and try and lead them away from the house. When you get an opportunity run to the back door. Marie will be waiting for you. Okay, here I go!"

Lucas shoved his way to the edge of the driveway, shading his eyes from the camera lights. It was impossible for him to hear one clear question, so he attempted to calm them down. He needed to be heard. He understood they had been cooling their heels for quite a while and he needed them on his side.

"Please, please, hold it down. I'll answer your questions one at a time, okay?"

"Mr. McNab, Mr. McNab, are you winning your case?" Several recorders appeared in front of his face.

"The trial isn't over yet, but we feel confident so far."

"What will the effect be on society if there is no such thing as murder?"

"Keep in mind, so-called murderers will not be set free. There can be all sorts of resulting charges levied by the courts. The fact is, we are attempting to prove that it is impossible to kill a person. As a learned man once said, 'When you die, you don't!'"

"Mr. McNab, you have made an impact all around the world. Are you concerned at all about the ramifications your assumptions might have on you, individually?"

"I haven't had time to consider anything like that. Please realize there is more to this than doing away with the charge of murder. We want people to understand more about our soul and what happens when we die. We want to dispel the fear of dying. We want to convey that the soul returns to God or whatever deity is worshiped. It returns to a wonderful afterlife to meet their loved ones who have passed on before. You all can help by being objective in your presentation of our evidence. Please try and do that. We urge folks to do research themselves. We are not alone in this. Keep an open mind."

The questioning continued for some time, with Lucas answering as many as he could. When he indicated he was through, the press had a different take on what was happening and a new respect for the man responsible.

When Lucas finally entered his house, he was met by loud applause.

"Well done, well done, Lucas! You were great! That will probably do more for us than the trial." Marie could hardly contain herself.

Ann gave him a long hug and a longer kiss.

"Thank you. Thank you. I'll admit, it was a lot better than I anticipated. They're only doing a pretty thankless job, after all. I don't care if it is early; let's have a tiny celebration!"

Later that evening after a late supper of Chinese food, Lucas, Marie, and Rosalie planned their morning testimony.

"I'm going to request that the court allow you to conduct a remote reading. I don't believe I will be refused. What all will you need to do this, Marie?"

"Just a small table and two chairs. It should only take a short time to prove the honesty of mediumship."

"Good. I'll check with the clerk and bailiff regarding a table. We'll have chairs. I'll put you on the stand first and establish some facts. I can't prepare you for testimony as you know far more than me, so like Simon and Andrew, I'll feed you some leading questions and give you your head, right?"

"Gotcha! Sounds like a fun morning. Andrew can attend court now, is that right?"

"We'll sit him with us and hope nobody notices. The place will be packed. Now, Rosalie. I want you at the very end. Of all the witnesses, the jury members will be able to relate to you. And again, preparation won't be necessary. I'll question you just like I did at your house. Remember?"

"Yes I do, Lucas. That will be alright then. My cousin is hoping to come and maybe some other people from Prospect will come too."

Marie and Andrew left for Dartmouth. Ann and Rosalie went off to their beds. Lucas ended up in the little 'war room' for a talk with Sarah.

"Hi, Hon. What do you think of the trial so far? I know you're right there at our table, probably giving advice we can't hear. I'm content with what I've done and I can do no more. Be with me tomorrow. Help and guide us. I love you."

Later that night in bed Lucas was still fitful, tossing and turning, playing different scenarios in his mind of next day's court. He wasn't aware of the bedroom door quietly opening and closing. He felt a change in the blanket at his back and a sudden breath of cool air. He carefully turned and found Ann's face on the pillow. She leaned in and kissed him.

"Pretend I'm thirty-five," was all she said.

• • • • •

The only change in the usual morning operation at the house was the attention Lucas paid to Ann. All three had a light breakfast, finishing with an extra coffee and the usual tea for Rosalie.

"My Ann, you look positively radiant this morning. You have lovely colour in your cheeks."

"Most likely the way I was sleeping, Rosalie. Thank you for the compliment," and she cast a sly look in Lucas' direction. He smiled.

"Alright, gang. This is it. Last day, let's enjoy it. How are you feeling, Rosalie? Ready for the battle?" Lucas asked.

"Oh, Lucas. I think we're going to do just fine. You just wait and see." Rosalie beamed.

This morning Lucas had decided that they would go in through the main entrance, through the crowd of clutching, grabbing press corps. Actually, they were quite restrained, opening up a path to the door. 'Maybe talking with them last night had been a good thing in more ways than one,' Lucas thought. He smiled and acknowledged several of the reporters. Andrew Cushing was doing everything he could think of to hide his face, hoping he would just appear to be part of the defence team, and it was working so far. Michael was already at his table. Lucas went to the clerk and asked about a small table. As he was walking back he passed close to Michael, who whispered, "Watch your back!"

Lucas looked over his shoulder at Michael, puzzled over his warning and what it could mean. Ann returned from the front hall and shielded Andrew from the prosecution table. Joseph was brought in, looking a little worse for wear, though he seemed his usual benign self. The public seating was filled to overflowing. Lucas noticed there was no sign of 'Mr. Black' this morning.

"All rise."

Judge Muirhead entered the courtroom, and Lucas immediately sensed something out of place with the judge.

"Court is now in session. The honourable Judge Muirhead presiding."

"Call your first witness, Mr. McNab."

Marie was called to the court and sworn in. She took her seat in the witness chair.

"Good morning Miss St-Onge. How are you this morning?"

"I'm fine, thank you."

"Miss St-Onge, you describe yourself as a psychic medium. In layman's terms, please, would you explain to the court exactly what that means?"

"Certainly. Psychic mediums have the ability to connect persons here on Earth with souls who have passed, or died, in earth terms."

"I see. How does this process take place? I'm sure most of us have difficulty understanding what you describe."

"I'll try and simplify the process for the court. Instead of getting messages from a phone or texts or tweets, mediums receive their messages through different psychic abilities. These various abilities are termed 'clairs'. I'll give you a few examples. Clairaudience refers to psychic hearing. For example, you suddenly hear in your head a voice saying, 'don't back up' and you discover a bicycle you would have run over. And there is claircognizance which is psychic knowing. This is when you get a strong feeling or premonition that affects your action, such as deciding not to drive a particular route because you determine it isn't safe. The last clair I'll mention is clairvoyance. Clairvoyance, which is my ability, allows me to receive direct messages by speech or other visuals, often I will receive images of the person I am channelling. That's the term for the reading. I see these in my head, in my 'mind's eye' I believe it to be the most common clair. I would venture to say some people here today are saying, 'Hey, that's happened to me!' and they would be correct. I believe we all have psychic abilities. We haven't tuned into them yet. It takes training. In truth, I'm just a messenger. I receive messages from someone on the other side and give them to a person living here. I am able to connect with souls who have crossed. It's that simple."

"You use the term 'crossed'. What do you mean by that?"

"When I say someone has 'crossed over', I am saying that person has reached the afterlife."

"Thank you, Miss St-Onge. You've explained it very well. I'll come back to the afterlife later."

There were some quick smiles, even from Lucas, when he realized what he had said.

"Please tell us how you come to have this special ability."

"I believe I was born with clairvoyance. As a child I had imaginary friends as many children claim. Parents are seldom aware of this taking place, and the child sees nothing out of the ordinary. Just friends to play with. It is believed that a child's mind is open to this type of event. Society hasn't yet set its claws into their brains. So they are receptive. As I grew older, these experiences faded but the ability remained. It just took a turn to clairvoyance. So I decided to follow it up and took training. Actually, I felt like I had no choice. Clairvoyance had chosen me. I trace it back to when I was a soul at the Source and there I took this upon myself as my mission, a part of my earthly education. My gift is helping me do this."

"You mention the Source. Would you explain that, please?"

"The Source, as we refer to it, has as many different names as there are religions. The Christian term would be God. The Source is the afterlife. As the name implies, it is the beginning. It is our home. And we experience a joyous reunion when we return home. Those of us who decided to come down here to this 'school' have very specific reasons for being here, and we have to find those reasons. Whatever they turn out to be they are designed to help mankind, and their main ingredients are love and peace. Let's say you have a great urge to write and you start down that particular passageway. There will be many choices you can make on how you complete this journey. That is your Free Will at work. I wish everyone here would make an effort to discover their mission here."

"Thank you. Did you take particular training to help you develop this gift you have?"

"Yes, I did. Early on, I was advised to attend a spiritualist church. Spiritualist churches are devoted to spiritual and psychic development. There are many across North America. I chose one in New Westminster, British Columbia. Various mediums are members, as am I, so it is a great opportunity to learn from experienced mediums. I also have a Bachelor of Metaphysical Theology."

"Now, Miss St. Onge, you are a firm believer in the soul, and we have learned a great deal about the soul from other witnesses. I want you to tell the court what you consider the soul to be and cite your proof that the soul exists."

"A man does not *have* a soul. You don't *have* a soul; I don't *have* a soul. We *are* souls that use the body to get around. Our souls run our body. Without a soul the body would be like a car without gas. The soul is the body's energy. Our soul gives us speech, hearing, sight, and thought. It is our identity, our personality, our intelligence, and our desires. Our soul is who we are. When the body dies our soul goes back home to the Source from whence it came and takes with it all those characteristics that were you. We are spiritual beings having an earthly experience. This is a testing ground for us to discover ourselves. There is a cosmic record being kept of all the things we do. How we conduct ourselves. Our loves and hates. No one is perfect, so we all have some black marks on our record along with the good.

"You ask me to prove that the soul exists. Isn't it strange, to see all the wonderful advancements technology has made to provide us a so-called 'better' life. Take the internet for example. Nearly everybody uses it for one thing or another. We send messages, receive mail, we can see who we talk to, we do our banking, income tax, play games. But does the everyday man or woman understand one iota of how the internet does all those things? Not on your life. We don't care to learn how it works; it just does, and we accept that. But when it comes to the soul... where's your proof? And even when proof is provided, we're still skeptical. So, I'll give you proof and I wonder how many will consider it? We already have to accept that the soul does not die. That has been proven... scientifically. Agreed? Where does the soul go after it leaves the body? Are there billions of souls just floating around out there somewhere, ducking space junk and bumping into each other? No! The soul goes home, as I stated before, to the Source. If that were not true I would not be able to connect to those souls who have gone home. And trust me, I have made contact with hundreds of them."

Lucas looked at Judge Muirhead and saw him wiping his forehead and drinking water. He looked to be in some distress. Lucas wondered why he didn't call a recess. He also couldn't understand why Michael was allowing him so much leeway. He hadn't objected to anything.

He seemed completely distracted, almost like he had lost interest in the trial. He motioned for Marie to continue.

"As for NDEs, these number in the thousands from around the world and a large number have been verified. Most have experienced some part of the afterlife, but science wants proof! They have come up with explanations of what *might* or *could* cause an NDE, none of which makes any sense. The skeptics have determined that what is experienced in an NDE is, now listen to this, a *socioculturally-determined hallucination*! That should turn folks away from the truth. It would me! It all boils down to this: if I can connect to a verified soul on the other side, what more proof is needed? I'll go out on a limb here and say I don't believe one debunker or non-believer has ever questioned my proof by being read themselves."

"Thank you for that. You've explained this very well. There is one last question, Miss St-Onge, if you would. Can you give us a glimpse into the afterlife?"

"Certainly. I have had three near-death experiences and I have experienced the afterlife somewhat. I was not permitted to enter fully the afterlife as I was told it was not my time. The first thing you notice is the light. It is so bright but at the same time it is not uncomfortable. The sky is beautiful shades of blue with fluffy white clouds with just a touch of yellow in them. The flowers are many and large, with the most vivid colours you can imagine! Lovely green grass everywhere, and the men will be pleased to hear it doesn't require mowing. I saw pathways everywhere. There are large inspirational buildings. I would sum it up this way; picture the most beautiful day you can remember, then multiply it ten times, maybe even one hundred times, and that would be the afterlife. I don't want to introduce vibrations except to say we all vibrate at a certain level. You might have said at one time that a particular person sends out bad vibes, something you feel about that person. The Beachboys had a hit with a song called *Good Vibrations,* didn't they? Our souls, in the afterlife, vibrate at a much higher rate and for them to make contact with me they must lower this rate tremendously and this depletes their energy and determines how long the session will be."

"I would like to add this, if I may. Our beliefs in no way impinge on orthodox religions. In nearly every facet we parallel them. We have only used modern techniques unknown to the writers of the Bible. I want that understood, please."

"One last question, please. In your opinion is it possible for one person to kill another?"

"No. It is not possible. The soul of a person never dies."

The crowded courtroom buzzed with astonishment and Judge muirhead rapped his gavel twice.

"Thank you so much, Miss St. Onge. You have been most helpful. Your witness, Mr. Sullivan."

The Crown prosecutor seemed anxious to question Marie.

"Hello, Miss St. Onge. I listened intently to your testimony. I only have a few questions for you. You say that what you are able to do, the readings and such, is a gift. It didn't cost you anything. You didn't have to buy it. My question is, do you charge customers? I expect you do. How can you charge for something you were fortunate enough to receive as a gift?"

Lucas was going to object until he noticed Judge Muirhead's obvious discomfort, and he let the question stay.

"You must remember, Mr. Sullivan, this is my vocation by which I make my living. I don't know what lawyers make per hour, but no doubt it is slightly more that the seventy-five dollars per session that I make. And I don't get to work eight hours a day either. I have never, ever had a person object to my charges. I am able to give them relief and peace of mind when their souls are troubled. You only get them money, or take their money it seems to me.

"Yes, well, I understand there are numerous frauds operating in your profession. How exactly does a person know if the medium across from him, or her, is for real or just a fake?"

A smile immediately crossed Lucas' face. He turned to Ann and whispered in her ear that Michael had just given him the opening he needed to have Marie do a reading. Lucas rose quickly to his feet.

"Your Honour, may I make a suggestion to the court? Miss St-Onge is willing to do a remote reading whereby she will read a person whom she can't see. She will only know that person's name and birth date. A tally can be made by the person being read and her accuracy determined. It will only take ten or fifteen minutes, twenty at the most, your Honour."

Judge Muirhead continued wiping his brow.

"Is the Crown in agreement?"

"We are, your Honour," answered Michael.

"Bailiff, Take the particulars from one of the security guards in the hall."

Lucas and Ann prepared the table the clerk had found and set it up on the floor so it was visible to the judge. Marie stepped out and took her seat at the table. The bailiff came back with the particulars which were checked by both Michael and Lucas and then passed to the judge.

When Marie received the paper, she held it with both hands, closed her eyes and was silent for several minutes. Then she began writing. She would sometimes take long pauses between her writing. Finally, she put down the pencil, leaned back in her chair, and closed her eyes again.

"This is all I can read from this person, your Honour."

Michael gave a shrug of his shoulders while smiling at Lucas.

"Bailiff, bring in the security guard."

"Mr. Caudell, would you please read what the lady has written as it relates directly to you? Please tell me the number of correct 'hits' and the number of 'misses'."

"Yes, your Honour." Caudell took Marie's paper and began reading and marking the paper.

When he finished he looked to the judge for what to do next.

"Well, Mr. Caudell, what is the tally?"

Again, the courtroom was deathly quiet. Every person including the jury members was leaning forward, not wanting to miss a word. Everybody wanted to be the first to hear the results. No one was more anxious than Lucas.

"Out of seventeen... comments, your Honour, thirteen were dead on, pardon the expression, two more I would have to check with family, and two were 'misses'." Mr. Caudell had a look of astonishment.

The exhaling could be heard as people sat back. There was only subdued chatter throughout the room.

"Let me see those results, Mr. Caudell." Caudell passed the results to the judge.

"Umm, that is very impressive Miss St-Onge. Mr. Caudell, is your middle name really Diogenes?"

Caudell was embarrassed. He looked at the floor as he answered the judge. "Yes, your Honour"

Does the Crown have any more questions of this witness?"

Michael responded in a low voice,"No, your Honour."

There was silence in the courtroom.

"No? Then court will recess until two this afternoon."

While everyone stood waiting for Judge Muirhead to retire to his chambers, his disappearance from view was accompanied by a large thump. Lucas rushed to the dias and found the judge crumpled to the floor. Michael was right behind Lucas and together they got the judge turned on his back. He was pale and his breathing was shallow.

"Bailiff, call 911 now! Emergency! Michael, look after the jury. They might as well go home. There will be no more court today."

Lucas loosened the judge's collar. Ann dampened a cloth with cold water and held it on the judge's forehead. She stayed with him until the ambulance arrived and the attendants took responsibility. Lucas and Michael cleared the press from the room. They had kept a respectful distance from all the activity. The courtroom was empty now, then in through the door came Rosalie. Everyone had forgotten about her.

"What in the world happened in here?"

Lucas explained what had taken place and seated her beside Joseph, who seemed oblivious to everything. His security officer wasn't much better. He stood close to Joseph in case he made a break for it, Lucas supposed. Rosalie smiled at Joseph and patted his hand. Marie stood talking to Mr. Caudell. Michael's assistant prosecutor, a pretty blonde lady, was sobbing and wiping her eyes. Andrew's head was on a swivel trying to watch everything and miss nothing. The tension was gone from the room and a tiredness was taking over.

Suddenly, Rosalie stood up, eyes wide, crying out... "'I'm not dead! I'm not dead!' Chuck is saying he's alive!"

Everyone turned and looked at Rosalie in stunned silence.

"What did you just say, Rosalie?" Lucas was afraid he had not heard correctly.

"This man, calls himself Chuck. He just came to me saying he wasn't dead."

"You said he called himself 'Chuck'?" Lucas couldn't believe this was happening.

"Yes, Mr. McNab. Chuck. The man said he was Chuck." Rosalie was adamant.

Lucas looked at Ann, then he looked at Michael.

"Who is she, Lucas?" Michael demanded.

"She's a medium from Prospect. I have been read by her. She's one of the good ones; don't worry, Michael. She was my next witness."

Rosalie was still standing and looking straight ahead.

"Now he's holding up his left hand. He's showing his two last fingers. They're half gone." Rosalie was holding up her left hand and covering the last two fingers with her right hand.

Now, as Joseph quickly stood up, the security officer was too slow to hold him in his seat.

"That's Chuck Conlon. I know. He lost them fingers cutting' up boxes for a fire. That's him. Hi, Chuckie boy, how ya doin'?"

Lucas turned to Michael. "Do you have the coroner's report here?"

"I think I do. Let me check. Yes, here it is. What are you looking for, Lucas?"

"Missing fingers."

Lucas studied the report, using his own finger like a cursor. Michael stood right beside him.

"Found them, right there, under distinguishing features. Bingo! My Lord, Michael, there's the proof! We don't die and we can't commit murder!" Lucas grabbed Michael by the shoulders and shook him. He then went over to Joseph Simpson, shook his hand, hugged him, and told him he had won. Joseph was only interested in where his friend Chuck was.

Marie gave Rosalie a big hug and congratulated her. Ann, with tears in her eyes, hugged them both. Andrew had a big smile on his face and slapped Lucas on the back several times.

The ambulance arrived and the attendants stabilized the judge, and carefully transported him to their vehicle. Everyone could only watch in silence as the judge left the courtroom... perhaps for the last time.

As the exuberance diminished Michael took Lucas aside, out of hearing range of the others, and spoke quietly but earnestly.

"Lucas, you were right about this whole thing, but the judge and jury are gone. And you're right when you say no trial today. There'll be no more trial. It's over. I'm the only proof you have that counts and I can't help you. Something very sinister has developed as a result of your defence and it is all-encompassing, right to the Chief Crown. This trial was never going to the jury. They, and we, both know who 'they' are, couldn't risk even a hung jury. They will stop at nothing to maintain the status quo. Judge Muirhead is just the first stage, God knows who's next, but they have to make it all go away, Lucas. The judge is just the first 'billboard' they'll put up saying 'That's what will happen to you if you don't stop thinking! Big Brother is watching.' I was warning you when I told you to watch your back. That's all I can tell you, Lucas. Your whole team should be extremely careful. Everything's up for grabs. Good luck."

Lucas stared into Michael's eyes as he listened to what he was saying. What *was* Michael saying? He always knew his defence strategy would be cause for concern in some quarters, but what kind of reaction was Michael talking about? This isn't some third world banana republic... is it? Michael was describing a third-rate B movie plot. He placed his hands on Michael's shoulders, still looking him in the eyes.

"Michael, if this is true, what you've told me, and I have to believe it to be, what have we become? This is Germany in the thirties, Russia under Stalin, America under... Thanks for the warning, Michael. You be safe too. Let me know about the judge if you find out anything."

Lucas shook Michael's hand long and hard. Michael took his briefcase and his co-council by the arm and left the courtroom. Those who were left of 'Lucas' team' gathered round him.

"What's going on, Lucas? You look like you've seen a ghost," Ann asked.

Lucas gave them the unbelievable news from Michael and the seriousness put them all in shock. Lucas knew he was responsible for putting them all in danger, and he had to have a plan of some sort to get them out.

"We have to leave the city as soon as possible. I don't think there will be immediate repercussions if there are even any, but better safe than sorry. I believe if they can shut down the mainstream media, which they can, that will buy us time to do what we have to do. Pack for a long trip. Carry cash, water, food, survival stuff. You know what you'll need. Before we break up, I just want you to know what a great job you've all done. We might have been able to change a lot of things for the good but it wasn't meant to be. I'm pleased to have met you all and I thank you for the bottom of my heart... my *soul*! I hope we can keep in touch and that we all have a wonderful life."

"Lucas, I'm proud to have been a part of all this. I wouldn't have missed it for the world! It's just like being home!" Everybody caught Andrew's meaning and laughed.

Lucas continued, "I wouldn't advise trying to cross the border for a while. I would suspect you, no, all of us have been flagged. Make Canada your home until things quiet down.

"Andrew, you and Marie might want to travel together for mutual support. I am really sorry I've put everyone in this situation. I know we'll come out the other end unscathed; just take precautions for a while. Thank you both and please, stay in touch." Lucas gave each a big hug.

"Well Rosalie, my dear. You were the 'star' of the show. I'm just so sorry the audience left so early!" They all had a good-natured laugh and closed in around Rosalie and hugged her.

"I owe you so much, Rosalie. You changed my life, you did, and look what it got me! You and your cousin get back to Prospect and hunker down. Please tell him I'm appreciative for his driving you. I wouldn't give a plug nickel for any outsider's survival if they tried to pull something there; I don't care what colour suit they wear! Be safe, Rosalie. I'll never forget you."

Tears were welling up in Rosalie's eyes. She had received a message but couldn't bring herself to tell them what it was. She gave them a little wave as she left the courtroom.

Marie went over to Lucas, put her arms around him, and kissed him.

"Meeting you, Lucas McNab, is something I'll never forget. I'll see you in the afterlife!"

Then there was just the two of them left. Ann's eyes were red from wiping tears away when each one said goodbye. She gathered up their papers and put them in her briefcase. Joseph was long gone, back to his warm cubbyhole in Dartmouth. Lucas looked back over the events that had taken place and felt like a director of a play on its final performance. 'Where were the flowers?' Lucas thought, giving himself a smile.

"Shall we go then?"

• • • • •

Blesse◆ is the influence of one true loving human soul on another.
- George Eliot

Lucas made a detailed sweep outside the house when they got back. He found nothing out of the ordinary and there was no sign of 'Blackie' either. As they let the warm, familiar atmosphere envelop them they relaxed for the first time that day, in each other's embrace. Lucas gave Ann a long, meaningful kiss, and nuzzled her neck. Her presence meant everything to him at this moment.

Neither wanted to break this spell of serenity after such a troubling day. Ann was the first to invade the quiet, whispering in Lucas' ear, "I would really appreciate a glass of wine, and I know what you want too."

"Well, right now I would settle for a large scotch."

They broke apart, and each made their own drinks. Their 'war room' was no more. It had returned to its state as their little oasis which they cherished more than ever. After several long minutes, each in his and her thoughts, Lucas looked at Ann.

"We've got to make plans, my dear, for getting out of Dodge. And it has to be done quickly.

Tell me what you think of this. Our vehicles are known, but nobody's seen Sarah's little Miata! So that's our car. Tomorrow you drive your Jeep to the apartment, pack what you want, and then call a taxi. Your address is known by now so you'll be watched, no doubt. Take a cab to the airport. Get a ticket to... oh, say, Montreal, or someplace that has a flight leaving around 10:30 or 11:00. Time all this so you won't have a long wait. Sit where there are lots of people around. I'll be there by ten or so. I won't let on I know you until the very end. When they call for boarding, get up and start walking toward the departure gate. That's when I'll pick you up and we'll quietly get to the car. I'm trusting that when they discover your plan to fly to Montreal, they'll leave. Try to disguise yourself a little too."

"Well, James Bond! You've got it all figured out, you have! Do you truly believe all this is necessary? Can't we just drive away? Into the sunset?"

"From what Michael told me, yes, what I've just laid out *is* necessary! He gave me reason to believe our lives could well be in danger. Mine anyway. And that brings up another thing. If you stay with me, you expose yourself to the same fate, and I love you too much for that. I just proposed a plan and took for granted you would be part of it, and that wasn't fair to you. Until you came to me and became part of me, I wouldn't have cared what the consequences would be. I probably would have embraced whatever befell me. Now, I love you and you have become a part of me, two souls joined at the heart, and that poses a problem. Now I care what happens to me."

"Lucas, Lucas, you mean the world to me. Even when Sarah was here I had feelings for you. Why do you think I never married? I wanted to stay a part of your life even if it would always be in the shadows. I love you too! And as far as I'm concerned where you go, I go, and the devil take the hindmost! It will always be us, together. Okay?"

Lucas went to Ann's chair, bent down and kissed her, and then drew back and looked into her eyes, those beautiful eyes that he had failed to notice for the past weeks. He leaned in again and kissed them both.

"We should get something to eat, my love."

"Something picky. I couldn't eat a big meal. What about you, Lukie, what would you like?"

"I think I'm with you. How about I do a tray of crackers, cheese, olives, and Polish sausage? Sound good?"

"Just the ticket." Ann snuggled into the warmth and happiness she felt.

That night they went to bed together and put the world away.

• • • • •

In the morning, along with the sun came the reality of the day. Neither of them ate much, just toast and coffee with a very large helping of apprehension. They had both decided that Lucas' plan from the night before would be the way to go. Lucas turned on the radio in the kitchen to get the local news. They listened closely but the only bit pertaining to yesterday was one referring to Judge Muirhead 'fainting' at the close of the morning session.

"Well, Michael was right. They got to the mainstream media. The only news we'll get now is what they want us to hear."

Just then Lucas' phone rang. It was Michael Sullivan.

"Hi Lucas. Everything alright? I'm calling on a landline afraid to use my cell. Isn't that bloody great? I've got some news on Judge Muirhead. He's in intensive care with, get this, 'an undisclosed virus'. Right. The flags are up and waving. Even the Chief is looking over his shoulder. Has anyone from the firm called to see how you are?"

"Not yet. Do you expect the judge to live, Michael?"

"No, I don't, Lucas. No, I don't. That would be a very loose end for them. I won't ask what your plans are. What I don't know shouldn't hurt me. Well, Lucas, I wish you and Ann all the luck in the world, and I'll see you... over there! Cheers."

"Cheers, Michael."

Lucas turned to Ann and gave her Michael's news. "I suppose we should start making tracks, love. Are you packed?"

"Pretty much. Let's have another coffee first." Ann hated to leave the house, especially not knowing when they would be back.

Lucas absently played the radio dial over the city stations, his mind on the coming events. A disembodied voice floated in the air as Lucas stopped 'surfing' the dial.

'This just in... a prisoner in the Dartmouth facility was found dead in his cell this morning. Joseph Simpson, accused killer of Charles Conlon earlier this month, apparently died from a heart attack. An autopsy will be performed according to the police. Now back to...'

Lucas, eyes wide in disbelief, took Ann in his arms. He knew now just how dire his straits were. Joseph's 'death' was not expected. They had thought he would be safe in jail for the rest of his life. This was a clear indication to Lucas of just how serious and dangerous these people are.

Ann's eyes filled, her tears showing what she felt in her heart. She looked up at Lucas, questioningly. "Lucas, what is happening? I'm frightened. Are they going to kill us all? Lucas?"

Lucas held her tighter. He could feel her tremble. He was cursing himself for ever starting this crusade. It was inevitable that they would come for him somewhere down the line. He was marked and now so was this beautiful lady in his arms. What had he done?

"Hush, shhhh, we'll soon be far away from all of this. Don't worry, my love. We'll be alright," Lucas lied. He gently rocked her back and forth until he could feel the trembling ease.

He wanted to protect her and keep her safe, keep them both safe, but he questioned being able to do that now. He didn't know who or how many were involved and at what levels of authority. In short, he knew next to nothing. The one thing he was sure of: he and Ann getting out of the city, *now!*

He held Ann at arm's length, smiled to ease her mind a little, and felt his love for her well up deep inside himself.

"We have to make our move, my sweet. Don't you worry; we'll make it okay. Do you remember everything you're going to do? Be strong, my girl. We'll soon be safely away from the madness, I promise."

"Okay, Lucas. I'll see you at the airport. Please don't leave me alone for long."

Ann picked up her small suitcase, kissed Lucas goodbye, and headed for the Jeep. Lucas watched from the door, waving as she swung unto the road, beseeching the powers of the Source to watch over and protect her. As he closed the door and prepared to start his part of their plan his phone rang. He didn't want to answer but thought better of it.

"Yes."

"Lucas... this is Matt. Are you alright? I've heard the news and I was worried about you and Ann. I followed the trial and you did a masterful job. Maybe too good. Even I, with all my connections, had no idea of the repercussions your evidence would cause. I should have. Is there anything I can do, Lucas?"

"Thanks for calling, Matt. Like you, I should have seen something like this happening. What in hell am I up against, Matt? I'm working blind here. I'll tell you one thing: Brannigan is up to his eyeballs in this. Don't trust him as far as you could throw the bastard. He was behind the scenes in the beginning, working on behalf of... who knows! Thanks for the offer of help, Matt. Gotta run. You won't be hearing from me. Cheers!"

Lucas packed a small bag with just essentials, enough for a few weeks which he thought would be sufficient. He would use the Equinox to get to the bank. He couldn't risk showing the Miata this early. Yellow stands out like a sore thumb. At the bank he withdrew all the cash, leaving just enough to cover the bills for one month. 'We'll be back by then,' he figured.

Returning to the house he parked the Equinox outside. He checked the gas and oil of the Miata since it had been sitting idle for over a year. Everything seemed fine. Would it start? He got in and turned the key... and the engine sounded as strong as ever! Everything was set. He threw his bag in the little trunk, put on his driving cap and sunglasses, raised the top of the Mazda to enclose the cockpit, turned up his collar, and headed to the airport.

He reached the airport just after ten o'clock. Entering the main concourse, he searched the people, looking for Ann. Then he panicked, remembering that he had mentioned a disguise. How would he find her? His looking became feverish. Was that her? No, not that one. 'Maybe if I walk around in the crowd she'll recognize me.' Ann saw him and stood up so Lucas could hopefully see her. He finally noticed her and nodded. A cursory look around at the passengers didn't expose anyone out of the ordinary. Finding an empty seat, he waited for Ann to make her move toward the security line-up and when she did, Lucas eased his way through the line until he was close enough to take her hand and they slowly made their way outside using the crowd of travelers as a screen. They crossed the approach road and found the Miata. Both travel bags were stored in the small trunk space. Lucas made one last serious survey of the parking lot and then eased into the driver's seat. Leaning over to Ann he gave her a kiss.

• • • • •

Neither of them had taken notice of a man seated outside Tim Horton's following their erratic movements. They hadn't seen him get up and follow them outside as they got into the little yellow car either. He quickly made a call.

"They are just leaving. They're driving a small yellow sports car."

• • • • •

"Well done, love. I wouldn't have recognized you with your hair tucked up under the tam like that. And where on Earth did you get those horrendous sunglasses!" Lucas smiled.

"I thought they were perfect. I figured they wouldn't expect someone going into hiding would be dumb enough to wear something so outlandish. How am I doing in this spy game?" Ann asked.

"You're doing just fine, my girl," he said as he patted her knee.

They drove out of the airport parking and turned on to the 102 toward Truro. They both relaxed, leaving much of the last few days behind. The Miata was fast and would take them far. They felt at ease for the first time in a while and smiled at each other.

"What are your plans, Lucas? Where are we going?"

"I think Cape Breton is the place for us to disappear. There are roads going everywhere. Friendly people, but suspicious too. What do you think of that?"

"It sounds like the place to be for sure. How long do you think we'll be away?"

"Oh, I don't know, Ann. Until this all blows over, I guess. Once it's off the front page, so to speak, we should be okay. Shouldn't be that long. Let's make a holiday out of it. We've earned it."

"Grand idea! Let's."

Lucas kept a wary eye on traffic behind him, but at his speed nothing was keeping up with him. He wished the car was a more subdued colour. 'Yellow is really loud,' he thought.

• • • • •

A black SUV was parked just off the Veteran's Memorial Highway at Enfield. A man was looking at an aerial view of a small yellow car booting it out of the city, heading north toward Truro. Zooming in with the drone's camera didn't disclose any more detail. As he watched the car weaving in and out of traffic, in his mind he ran through all the possible destinations the car could have. New Brunswick? Possible. It's the route to the rest of Canada and points South. Prince Edward Island? Too small. No place to hide. Cape Breton? There were options there. Easy to lose yourself and people to count on. Newfoundland ferry? Another island, but again the type of people that could make it impossible for him to be effective in what he had to do. He felt certain the car would stay in Cape Breton. Reaching for the controls of the drone, he turned it and brought it back to the vehicle. 'What will they think of next?' he asked, as he looked at the drone in wonder and packed it away with his other equipment. He headed the SUV to Truro, keeping the yellow car in sight.

• • • • •

They got to Truro about noon so they decided to have lunch. Turning off on Robie Street, Ann thought Frank and Gino's looked interesting, so Lucas pulled in the parking area. He quickly exited the car and took a look around. Again, he saw nothing suspicious. The restaurant was a hubbub of activity this time of day indicating it was a popular eating place.

It took a few minutes but they were eventually seated.

"This is nice, eh, Lucas? We're in no great hurry, are we?"

"No, we are not, my love. We're going to have a nice relaxing meal. Have you checked the menu yet?"

"Well, the cranberry chicken caught my eye. I believe I'll have that."

"Sounds like a good choice. Me, I'm having the maple whiskey salmon. Ummm!"

"And shall we have wine, my good man? I'd like to try the Jost Tidal Bay."

"And you shall have it, my good woman!"

Lucas took Ann's hands in his and they smiled at each other with both their lips and their eyes. 'This was love again,' Lucas admitted, and he knew how fortunate he was to have discovered it a second time. Then, mindful of his wife's warning, he assured Sarah he still belonged to her.

They left the restaurant. Lucas searched out a gas station for a fill-up, then drove back on the road that would take them to their sanctuary.

They had not seen any evidence of being followed. Lucas cautiously assumed that enough had been accomplished with the judge and poor Joseph Simpson and they wouldn't bother with him and Ann.

The black SUV had been parked in an adjacent business where an eye could be kept on the Miata. There were several roads leaving Truro resulting in the driver needing to stay closer to his quarry. Once their direction was determined, he would fall back at a safer distance.

"I wonder how everybody is making out," Ann wondered.

"I was wondering the same thing just now. Lord, I hope they all made it out of the city. Simon would have the hardest time, not being familiar with the country at all. Marie would take care of herself and Andrew okay, I think, and Rosalie would be bunkered up in Prospect, safe from everything but an aerial attack!"

"Have you given thought to where we'll spend the night?"

"Not really. We can easily make the island before nightfall. We'll find something there. We're going to take our time, Ann. This is our vacation and we're going to enjoy every minute of it. Right?"

"Absolutely!"

"See if you can find any city news on the radio, could you, please?"

Ann ran the dial up and down slowly until she tuned in to a CBC station, and left it there.

The road was good and fast until they reached the New Glasgow bypass where it changed into the 104, still an excellent road. They bypassed the university town of Antigonish and drove on to the Causeway. The little Miata crossed the short iron bridge that spanned a canal and continued to the sweeping curve of the land bridge that took them to Cape Breton. Lucas recalled the slogan with a chuckle, 'Down with Da Causeway, Byes', as he left the mainland.

They stopped at a tourist bureau to stretch their legs, get a cold drink, and pick up a map. The weather was ideal, warm with little wind, unusual for Cape Breton this early in the year. Going to the trunk of their car, they spread out the map, located their position, and decided to stay on the 104 to St. Peter's and see what was there.

They found St. Peter's was a bustling community with all the amenities. Driving slowly down the main street, keeping an eye out for accommodations for the night, Ann almost envied the residents.

"What a lovely, quiet place, Lucas. I could live here quite nicely, thank you. It has everything you would need and it's close to the water."

Lucas, looking around, just nodded his head in agreement. Reaching the edge of the commercial part of the village they saw a sign advertising an inn. Lucas quickly backed up so he could read it.

"Bras d'Or Lakes Inn. What do you think, Ann? Shall we give it a go?"

"It looks like a really nice place, Lucas. Let's."

They were completely taken with the cedar logs, exposed ceiling rafters, and subdued wall lighting. The interior exuded atmosphere and Ann was taken in with it all. Lucas was fortunate to obtain a room and they quickly settled in. Welcome showers and a change of clothes did wonders for both. A meditative stroll around the grounds set the mood for a long, relaxing meal in the rustic dining room.

They lingered over their wine, so at ease with each other now. Conversation centred around the wonderful relationship that Sarah, Lucas, and Ann had shared over the years. The tension and pressure from the last few weeks was easing and the soothing, loving bond between Lucas and Ann was beginning to allow the natural, pent-up emotions so long buried under personal obligations to surface. Their souls were experiencing a softer kind of love, deeper and more meaningful than young love, and both were so thankful that it had found them.

They finally left the table and decided to take another stroll, hand in hand, in the fading light of day. Ann nestled against Lucas' shoulder as they walked through the twilight. Back in the foyer Lucas bought a *Herald* newspaper and they went up to the room. It was quite natural now for them to be together in a bedroom. They lay on the king-sized bed and Ann turned on the TV to find some news while Lucas scanned the newspaper for any clues that might tell them something, anything, about the judge, the trial, any little detail. They found nothing, anywhere. Then his phone rang.

"Yes," he answered cautiously.

"Lucas? This is Marie. Are you okay?"

'It's good to hear your voice, Marie. Everything okay? Don't tell me where you are."

"We're doing fine. No problems so far. You?"

"We're good. Nothing to report. Any news on the judge?"

"He died, Lucas. One brief mention a few days ago on the news and nothing since."

There was a long pause on Lucas' end.

"Stay well, Marie, you and Andrew. Be careful. Love you both."

Lucas told Ann about the judge. Nothing further was said.

Lucas walked to the window and stared at the ocean in the waning light. He felt empty and, for the first time, frightened. He had to pull himself together for Ann's sake. She was sitting on the bed, her head lowered and her eyes closed. He knew what she was thinking. 'My God, what have I done?' Nothing was worth what he was putting her through. He reached for her hands, cold hands, and brought them up to his face. She raised her head and smiled at him.

"It's alright, Ann. Don't worry. We're safe. Nothing will happen to us. It's all over."

Ann gave him another smile, but her eyes, those windows to her soul, showed fear and apprehension. He kissed her still cold hands.

That night, in the king-sized bed, they held each other in a close, warm embrace, eventually sharing a troubled sleep until early morning.

They awoke to find the dawn already up and promising a bright, new day. Both were feeling better and looking forward to a hearty breakfast.

Lingering over a second cup of coffee, the conversation ultimately turned to how everything had gone so wrong.

"It's certainly been covered up nicely. There's been some high level, or more likely clandestine forces at work here. You know, Ann, I'll put money on the fact that the Prime Minister or the President or any other head of state doesn't have a clue as to what is taking place. This has to have been a 'black Ops' operation all the way. I can't see it from any other perspective."

"I realize that what you presented to the public through the trial, if allowed, would have created all sorts of problems for society. We discussed this very thing a while back. I think you're absolutely right to suspect 'black Ops', as you call them. You really rocked the boat and we were lucky to escape the madness. One benefit I got out of it, I found love again!"

• • • • •

The man in black slept in the SUV in a picnic area outside Port Hawkesbury and was up early. He had to locate that yellow car, and soon. He took out the specialized drone and controls and prepared it for flight. The farther up the island, the harder it would be to find them. Route 105 was a good bet and it was searched first. Nothing showed up on the small screen. Next, he tried Route 19 with the same results. 'They spent the night in some nondescript little B&B, no doubt.' He sent the drone West, along Route 104. Not a yellow car to be seen, anywhere. Now he was getting concerned. Wait, what was that. There. Right there in the front parking lot. The yellow car! He got out the map and located St. Peter's. That's got to be the place. He took the drone down quickly to a level where he could read the sign. Bras d'Or Lakes Inn.' He brought the drone back, stored it and looked for a place that served breakfast. Over a plate of eggs and ham and two cups of black coffee he tried to imagine their route from the Inn. He was confident they wouldn't backtrack. They would head up Route 4, taking them to Sydney. Sydney! The ferry terminal. Maybe they *are* heading to Newfoundland. He would have to stay closer to them now.

• • • • •

In a world where everyone wears a mask, it is a privilege to see a soul.

After a substantial breakfast, Lucas paid the bill and they started their journey again. In the car he showed Ann where he proposed to go that day, following Route 4 to the Eskasoni turn off, a couple of short ferry rides to the 105 to Baddeck.

"It's another great day, gorgeous. Today should be a beautiful drive, right along the shore of Bras d'Or Lake."

"I really love this country Lucas. Can't we stay?"

"We'll discuss that over wine one of these nights. Ready to go?"

Lucas had stored the hardtop and they enjoyed the wind in their hair and the fresh smell of the land and sea. The lake was calm and the gulls were soaring above the surface, searching for their breakfast. Lucas was in no hurry to put this day behind them. He was savouring every moment, capturing images in his mind, creating memories. They were approaching Big Pond.

"Oh, look, Lucas! There's Rita's tea room. Did you see it?"

"Yes, I did. We don't drink tea or I would have stopped."

"We do so drink tea, you." Ann gave him a slap on the arm.

He smiled at her and thanked the powers that be that they were together. At the U-turn to Eskasoni he slowed down more as the road had deteriorated and it ran very close to the water.

At the Grand Narrows they had to wait for the little ferry to come back so they got out and stretched their legs, marveling at the clear blue sky.

• • • • •

The black SUV was parked off road at Ben Eoin. The driver flew the drone up Route 4 to verify the Miata was continuing to Sydney. With the drone at several hundred feet above the road he thought he noticed what could have been the Miata traveling down the other side of East Bay. He took a closer look and saw it was the target vehicle. With the top off it had been difficult to pick up the car on the screen. 'He's not going to Newfoundland after all! He's driving like he's on his honeymoon!'

• • • • •

Soul meets soul on lovers' lips.
- Percy Bysshe Shelley

"Oh, look, Lucas. Someone's flying one of those drone things. Probably making a documentary or something."

Lucas shaded his eyes to have a look at the drone and noticed it was larger than he thought drones to be. The ferry arrived and carried them across the channel, and within a very short time they were taking another ferry at Little Narrows. The drive up to Baddeck was also along the lake edge and Ann was in a world of her own, happier than she had been in a very long time.

Lucas drove through the village, taking side roads and looking the place over. 'What a pretty village,' he thought. They passed colourful little eating places and gift stores. In the bay were anchored dozens of sailboats, their white sails glistening in the light.

"The population here most likely doubles in full summer," Ann mused.

Lucas remembered passing an interesting looking building called the Telegraph House and Motel. It was on a rise of land and he thought it might be a good place for a meal. He found it again, drove up, and parked.

"What's this, Lucas?"

"I thought we might try the fare here tonight. Are you game?"

"As long as I'm with you, I'm game for anything!"

"Ummm! I might hold you to that, my girl."

Sitting at the last unoccupied table on the deck, both enjoyed a delicious meal. It was too late to drive so Lucas booked a room. A leisurely walk down along the waterfront watching the evening glow fade upon the water closed a perfect day. The lovers ambled back to their room, with Ann holding firm to Lucas' arm, feeling safe and full of love for this man. She would be his for all time. Then an image of Sarah came to her mind and she added... 'while here on Earth!' and she smiled inwardly.

The following morning after breakfast they made the short walk to the Alexander Graham Bell Museum and spent a couple of hours learning about the great innovator that was Bell. Then it was back in the *yellow submarine,* as Ann called the Miata, to continue their trip around the Trail. It was a spectacular drive with vistas of sea and coast that made them marvel at the splendour of it all. Ann sat back and let the glory of the morning consume her senses. Lucas chose to drive the 205 which paralleled the Trans Canada because it stayed close to the water and he knew Ann would enjoy it. He turned left on MacDonald Road and took a short drive to connect to the 105. Finally, they turned onto the Cabot Trail, eagerly anticipating the advertised beauty of the Trail. After passing North River Bridge they marvelled at the beauty spread out before them. Passing through small villages and coves they could only imagine the life of these hardy people. Lucas had a better understanding of the pride of Cape Bretoners.

The Trail cut across the top of the Island and defined the northern boundary of the National Park then turned south down the western coast.

"I imagine fall colours are beautiful. It would be fun to come to the Celtic Colours some year, Lucas, wouldn't it? All that great music. One great big kitchen party."

"It would be fun. Want to come back in the fall?" Lucas offered.

"Let me get over this trip first before I answer that," Ann answered him, laughing.

"I think Cheticamp is a good stop to break up the trip," Lucas suggested.

"I think so too. I'm hoping we get closer to water on this side of the island. We can see what's there for accommodations. Since it will be our last night on the Trail, let's get something really nice."

"We'll get the best they have."

They decided the Auberge Baywind Suites was the place for them. It had an ocean view and an enticing place to eat, the Harbour Restaurant and Bar. As it was early for the tourist season, Lucas was able to have the Queen Suite, advertised as 'perfect for a romantic getaway'.

"Ann... would you say we qualify for a 'romantic getaway'?"

"What are you talking about - a romantic getaway?"

Lucas picked Ann up and danced around the room singing a Neil Young song. 'Out on the Trans Canada Highway there was a girl hitch-hiking with a dog...'

They were late for dinner, choosing a table for two in front of a window framing the waters of the cold Atlantic. While lingering over drinks, conversation was replaced with subtle expressions of love and affection. They were two people experiencing a truly 'romantic getaway'!

They both decided on the local snow crab, passed on dessert, but had coffee.

After eating they took a leisurely, hand in hand stroll around the water side of the restaurant.

Returning to the suite, Lucas rummaged through his carry-on bag and came up with a bottle of white wine. Opening it, he heard Ann exclaim in surprise, "Where did you get that, Lucas McNab!"

"I've carried it all the way from the city, I'll have you know. I was aging it on the Cabot Trail."

Lucas poured two glasses and took them out to the small balcony. Ann followed him. They touched glasses and kissed. No two people could have been happier at that moment.

About that time a large black SUV eased into the parking area, far away from the Miata.

• • • • •

A morning soak in the bathtub and the buffet breakfast set them up for the last part of the Trail. The morning was overcast with clearing skies promised later on. Lucas settled up at the front desk and they made their way out to the car. As he stored their cases in the little trunk, he happened to notice the black SUV. It startled him somewhat but he quickly passed it off to coincidence. As they pulled onto the highway, the driver of the SUV quickly got in and started the engine. He let the yellow car drive out of site before entering the main road.

"Now this is what I expected the whole drive to be like. Open ocean all the way!" Ann had a perfect view and was savouring every moment.

Traffic was extremely light, but Lucas was in no hurry. He thought, 'if we lived here we'd be home now'. He was passing through Grand Etang when he saw the SUV in the mirror.

It was getting closer and Lucas became concerned. Why would this be happening now? Maybe it wasn't him at all. Could just be tourists or even somebody local, maybe. But the ominous black vehicle was really close now. What was he planning to do? Lucas touched Ann on the shoulder and told her to hold on and stay low. He stepped on the gas and the little yellow car sped away, but the SUV stayed with it.

Here the road hugged the rocky coastline. The SUV pulled alongside the Miata. The driver looked over at Lucas as Lucas looked at him. Then the man in black turned the SUV quickly and hard into the little car. The Miata hurtled over the low guard rail and somersaulted to the rocks below, finally pitching into the cold, dark Atlantic. The black vehicle with a smudge of yellow paint on the front right fender roared off down the road.

No other vehicles passed the damaged guard rail for some time. Floating on the water below was a travel brochure - *Come Sea Beautiful Cape Breton.*

• • • • •

Nowhere can a man find a quieter or more
untroubled retreat than in his own soul.
- Marcus Aurelius

Lucas floated as if he were weightless. He could barely make out the dull yellow of the Miata through the dark blue water. 'What happened? Where's Ann? I've got to find Ann.' Was he having a near-death experience? No, this felt more final than that. All of a sudden, he was ascending at great speed to what appeared to be a tunnel. Yes, he was going into a big, black tunnel and he heard the most beautiful, celestial music all around him. 'Are those angels beside me? They seem to be guides, helping me along.' Each one took Lucas gently by the arm and led him toward a stunning bright light at the far end. 'The light is so bright! But it doesn't hurt my eyes. There appear to be people standing in the light. Who are they? Are they waiting for me? Where am I going?'

As they approached the light Lucas could make out faces of people he thought he knew. 'That looks like Mom and Dad, but they look so young.' They were holding each other and smiling warmly at Lucas.

'Is that Sis? It is! She looks just the same as I knew her before she passed.' She was jumping up and down and clapping her hands in excitement. Then, from the back, as the people moved aside, came a lady he would always know, his Sarah. She was radiant and looking younger than he remembered. She laughed and held out her arms toward him. 'Sarah, is it really you?'

He heard her voice in his head saying, 'Yes Lucas. It's me. I've been waiting for you.' Lucas timidly stretched out his hand to touch her and see if she was real. He delicately placed a finger on her cheek and felt her person.

'You *are* real! Really, really real!' Suddenly it hit him: he was talking, but his lips weren't moving! It was all taking place in his head! Thought transference? 'What's next?' he wondered.

Just then an unknown force calmly directed him to an enclosed space where his whole life on Earth was shown as in a sped-up movie and he was evaluated. His life on Earth was judged - the good that had been accomplished against the not so good things done throughout his allotted time. It was deemed that Lucas had illustrated purpose and meaning and love during his lifetime and had shown great compassion. Like a pilgrim, he had suffered in his attempt to show the way. He was accepted to the third level. When instructed to chose an age for himself, he indicated he wanted to be the same age as Sarah. And it was done. He asked this Source, as it was called, about Ann, and was told she was going through the same evaluation in another location and would have her friends and family around, especially a friend with a motorcycle. He was then allowed to join his family again and there was a joyous reunion. Relations he had only known about as a result of his research into the family genealogy were all there, showing appreciation for keeping them 'alive' for future generations. He hugged his parents and sister and as many relatives as he could. Sarah he hugged and kissed. He couldn't take his eyes off of her, forgetting how devastating her illness had been. As a group they walked Lucas into the world of the Afterlife.

R . B . B r o w n

The whole visible world was bathed in that wondrous light that had no discernable source. The feeling of love, pure unconditional love, was palpable. This area was like a park in a city. He walked through beautiful green grass, greener than he had ever seen. He observed gravel pathways going everywhere with the most exquisite, vibrantly-coloured, huge flowers growing as they walked past them with hundreds of butterflies fluttering about and birds of every description flying here and there. Trees with flowers blooming were everywhere. It seemed to Lucas that every living thing was celebrating his arrival.

They came to buildings of indescribable beauty of design that appeared to be made out of pure white alabaster and glass, reaching up into the dark blue sky with its white and pink fluffy clouds. Here, he was told, you could learn anything in which you had an interest. Lucas saw people coming and going just like on Earth. He was told that everything on this astral plane was as solid as it would be on Earth and the plane was a parallel to the Earth's universe. Here his family and all the others left he and Sarah alone, waving and smiling as they disappeared in a wink of the eye. Lucas was astonished. There was so much to learn. So much to understand.

Sarah took his hand and they left at 'thought speed' to beautiful snow-capped mountain ranges, tall forests, rivers and lakes, thunderous waterfalls, and wildlife of many kinds. They swooped and sailed above all the beauty one could imagine, both laughing and back in love. Eventually they came down to Earth near a lovely little blue-green lake with a little cabin nestled on the shore, a wharf running out into the calm waters where a beautiful red canoe lay waiting.

"This is where we live, Lucas. We've been waiting for you, the cottage and I. Welcome home!"

The End

Dedication

To the soul of my dear wife, Shyrlie, who was so instrumental
in the writing of this novel; to our wonderful children,
Vicki, Lori, and Terry; and lastly to Rita Crosbie, a medium's
medium who opened my mind to an exciting new world.

Acknowledgments

I owe a great big thank you to our daughter, Lori Ann, who gave me feedback as I wrote this story.

She read it in sections and is really looking forward to reading the whole piece in its proper form! Lori also contributed the title, *Soulitude*, which is so appropriate.

Another big thank you must go to Rita Crosbie for writing the forward for the book, who was so helpful in accommodating my frequent requests for readings and her ability to channel Shyrlie so well. Rita has done readings for family members across Canada. She can be reached at: www.soundbeings.com.

I recommend the following websites which have free newsletters:

SOUL PROOF newsletter
Mark Pitstick, MA, DC
www.soulproof.com

AFTERLIFE-EVIDENCE
www.victorzammit.com

About the Author

R. B. Brown (Blair) was born in Selma, Nova Scotia, on May 24th, 1936. He grew up in the Windsor - Falmouth area of the province. His first cousin, Harry Brown Junior, was an author and screenwriter, and had a movie made from his book *A Walk In The Sun*. Blair began his writing career quite early by writing what he thought was happening between the scenes in comic books.

He and Shyrlie married in 1956 and have three children.

Blair is a retired Industrial Arts teacher now living in Barrington Passage, Nova Scotia. He and his family have lived in Quebec, Ontario, Lesotho, S. A., Tanzania, E. A. and Jamaica, W. I. They have also traveled through Europe and had extended stays in Botswana, Southern Africa; and Athens, Greece.

Music has always been 'instrumental' in Blair's life, having had his own three-piece band. He is also a professional pyrographer. His work can be seen on Google - *Blair Brown Pyrography*.

Soulitude is Blair's first novel.